WILSON AT VERSAILLES

58579

INTRODUCTION

NO document composed in the twentieth century has generated greater or more enduring controversy than the Treaty of Versailles. The reasons are clear enough. Never did the peoples of the earth hope for so much from so few as they did from Woodrow Wilson and his colleagues at the Paris Peace Conference in 1919. Never before or since have statesmen managed to embody in a single agreement so many specific provisions affecting all quarters of the globe. Never has so broad a peace settlement been followed so rapidly by revolutionary changes within nations, by severe economic depression, and by a still more devastating world war. Questions have been inevitable. Did the diplomats at Paris unnecessarily frustrate the hopes of the world? To what extent was the Versailles settlement responsible for the tragic events of later years? Inevitably, too, the increasing urgency of diplomatic problems in our time has provoked fresh evaluations of this effort to construct a new international order. It is not surprising that the judgments have been diverse, that the controversy has been heated, and that the issues remain vitally relevant to our present concerns.

Dispute over the treaty began as soon as its terms became public. Germans and many liberals in the Allied Countries protested that the provisions were too harsh, a "Carthaginian peace," not only unjust in light of the Armistice terms but impossible of fulfillment and productive only of future discord and war. Numerous Frenchmen and aroused citizens elsewhere countered that the treaty was in actuality too soft upon the Germans since it did not give France all those guaranties of security which her leaders had requested. A third verdict asserted that there were only two practical alternatives for treating a defeated enemy, either extreme indulgence which would leave no grievances or extreme ruthlessness which would permit no possibility of retaliation. But the Treaty of Versailles achieved neither. This peace, ran one classic comment, was too weak for the harshness it contained.

Beyond the "hard-soft" category of dispute another cycle of criticism has been devoted to the question of whether the settlement embodied too utopian a "new order" or maintained too reactionary an "old order." The treaty's greatest weakness, some have charged, lay in its lack of political realism. By pursuing the principle of self-determination it created too many weak nations in central Europe. It substituted for older considerations of the balance of power a mistaken faith in the new League of Nations. It abandoned the tested principles of diplomacy which had limited warfare in Europe during the nineteenth century for untried, idealistic arrangements which led to world war within a generation. Other critics, however, have protested that far from establishing a New Order the treaty simply restored

not come to share their disappointment with Wilson's procedure at Paris. In these pages Wilson emerges as a remarkably effective negotiator and the treaty as a reasonable embodiment of his program.

America's entry into this second world war brought increased concern for the peace that would follow. Historians (and President Roosevelt himself) looked anxiously at Wilson's experience in an effort to gain perspective upon present problems and to avoid the mistakes of the past. Thomas A. Bailey, long a scholar in the diplomatic field, consciously strove in 1944 to distinguish the avoidable from the unavoidable difficulties of peacemaking by studying the proceedings in 1919. Like the authors of the previous selections, Bailey largely accepted Wilson's program as desirable and concentrated attention upon the methods of negotiating the treaty. President Roosevelt, by insisting upon unconditional surrender, by encouraging bipartisanship, by separating the United Nations from any particular peace treaty, attempted to profit from his own conception of Wilson's tactical errors.

At the same time, however, our involvement in another world war and then in the complexities of cold war diplomacy led many American intellectuals to question more seriously the adequacy of Wilson's whole approach to international affairs. Many of the criticisms they now espoused had been raised earlier but seemed to have gained greater significance in the uneasy years of the nineteen-forties and fifties. As a result, these critics turned their attention away from the procedural aspects of Wilson's diplomacy at the Peace Conference in order to debate the general outlines of his program.

Drawing upon comments about the Treaty of Versailles made from a socialist viewpoint by E. H. Carr, Richard Hofstadter stressed the economic limitations of the President's Fourteen Points. In this, Hofstadter went beyond Keynes's critique of the treaty's economic provisions to charge that Wilson's program did not mitigate the commercial and industrial rivalries between nations or the economic privileges within nations which were basic sources of discontent and war.

A young Frenchman, on the other hand, emerged to defend Wilson and the treaty for its economic arrangements only to find that "the political defects were the really decisive ones." Etienne Mantoux, son of a member of the French delegation in 1919, wrote his book (subtitled *The Economic Consequences of Mr. Keynes*) primarily to demolish the earlier contentions of Keynes. Mantoux argued at length not only that Keynes had been mistaken but that his attack upon the treaty had encouraged American isolationism and weakened resistance to Hitler's advances. Insofar as any fault could be found with Wilson and the treaty, Mantoux felt that it lay in the conscious rejection of concern for the balance of power, in the creation of many small, strategically indefensible states, and in undue reliance upon the League of Nations.

Walter Lippmann, also, in a book which undertook during the war to chart a course for future American foreign policy, found Wilson's conception of the League unrealistic and misleading. Only firm, specific alliances among the great powers could be trusted to insure collective security. The League was simply a device which kept Wilson from facing the necessity for such alliances.

This emphasis by writers like Mantoux and Lippmann upon power factors in diplomacy foreshadowed the most re-cent debate among students of Ameri-can foreign policy. The pressures of atomic threat and Soviet challenge have evoked an intense examination of the traditional assumptions behind our di-plomacy. The result has been a profound and far-reaching controversy between the advocates of "realism" and the pro-ponents of "idealism" in our foreign policy. In many ways this debate raises more fundamental questions for Ameri-cans than earlier disputes over imperial-ism *versus* anti-imperialism or isola-tionism *versus* internationalism. The so-called "realists" express concern over the national proclivity for "crusades" to save the world for democracy, the tend-ency of Americans to view foreign affairs in highly moralistic terms, and our in-clination to expect too much of interna-tional law and international organiza-tions. They urge greater attention to power balances in the anarchic interna-tional arena, increased reliance upon limited but more possible goals in for-eign policy, more recognition of the limi-tations as well as the possibilities of old-fashioned diplomacy. About all that Americans can really hope to understand and perhaps to achieve in foreign affairs, they argue, is our own national interest.

To "idealists" this train of thought seems not only dangerous but also an abandonment of the highest tradition in American foreign policy. In their eyes, to lose faith in the possibility of international law and to desert the prin-ciple of an international organization where great and small states alike de-cide the affairs of the world is to fore-swear America's unique federal, demo-cratic contribution to the world and to consign ourselves to power struggles whose end can only be the futility of war.

The debate has often reached a high level of abstraction and sophistication. Its fundamental importance, however, can best be seen when applied to the understanding of some particular foreign policy issue. The peace program of Woodrow Wilson in the first World War is an issue which has clearly separated the "realists" from the "idealists." For George Kennan the "legalistic-moralis-tic" approach of Wilson to the problems of that conflict embodied all that he finds most reprehensible in American thinking about foreign policy. On the other hand, Frank Tannenbaum argues in the final selection that Wilson may have failed to make the League and the Treaty all it should have been, but Wil-son's peace program represented what is best and most distinctive in the Amer-ican tradition. Only by some form of in-ternational "coordinate state" can we hope for peaceful solution of the world's problems.

Today, the problems of diplomacy and of the kind of world order for which we should strive are more pressing and more inescapable than ever before. We have achieved the preeminent position of leadership in the free world, but at the same time we are experiencing an unprecedented sense of insecurity and frustration in international relations. Where are we to lead? What are our goals in world affairs, and by what meth-ods are they to be achieved? Woodrow Wilson conceived in 1919 a vision which inspired and has continued to inspire many Americans as the best hope for a troubled world. Wilson shouldered the chief responsibility for framing the Treaty of Versailles along the lines of that vision. Was his conception faulty? Did he betray his own best ideals amid the insistent pressures of the Peace Con-ference? For three decades and longer,

REAR VIEW

—Orr in the Chicago *Tribune*

BLOWING BUBBLES

—Munson in *The American Economist*

YOU CAN'T REALLY BLAME HIM
FOR WANTING A LIFE PRESERVER

—Reid in *The National Republican*

TOWSER'LL SEE HE STAYS PUT

—Pease in the Newark *News*

THE CLASH OF ISSUES

Did Wilson betray his own program for peace?

"Of President Wilson's twenty-three conditions, only four can, with any accuracy, be said to have been incorporated in the Treaties of Peace. . . . The collapse of President Wilson at the Paris Peace Conference is one of the major tragedies of modern history. To a very large extent that collapse can be attributed to the defects of his own intelligence and character."

—HAROLD NICOLSON

"A careful study of the record reveals an extraordinary consistency in Wilson's fight for his program under overwhelming difficulties, as well as a high degree of political intelligence in translating the abstract principle of his program into concrete details of application."

—PAUL BIRDSALL

Was Wilson's peace program itself faulty?

"Conspicuously absent from the Fourteen Points was any meaningful demand for a substantial change in international economic relations. . . . The treaty and the League Covenant were an attempt, in the language of democracy, peace, and self-determination, to retain the competitive national state system of the nineteenth century without removing the admitted [economic] source of its rivalries and animosities."

—RICHARD HOFSTADTER

". . . while the economic defects of that settlement were, for the most part, illusory or exaggerated, the present writer shares the view of those who have maintained that the political defects were the really decisive ones. . . . in the failure, and one might almost say in the deliberate failure, to establish a true *balance of power*."

—ETIENNE MANTOUX

"Wilson identified collective security with antipathy to alliances, rather than with the constructive development of alliances."

—WALTER LIPPMANN

What should be the principles underlying American foreign policy?

"I see the most serious fault of our past policy formulation to lie in something that I might call the legalistic-moralistic approach to international problems."

—GEORGE F. KENNAN

"Now the advocates of *Realpolitik* would sweep away all of our old beliefs as foolish, sentimental, and moralistic. They would have us build our future upon the concept of the balance of power in international relations, throw all morality and law out of the window as a hindrance and nuisance to skilled diplomacy."

—FRANK TANNENBAUM

the general nature of the contents of at least the European ones—they were published in the press in November—and had apprised the President; and Secretary of State Lansing knew at least of the Anglo-Japanese accord of 1915 with regard to the conquered German islands in the Pacific. These treaties, which molded the final peace, were not so bad as some publicists have painted them. It is instructive to note that where they were followed there was no sore point left in the subsequent peace settlement. Students of the war have excoriated the treaties as proof of the naked imperialistic designs of the Allies as contrasted with the hypocrisy of their professions of fighting for the defense of democracy and the rights of small nations. That the treaties were tinctured with imperialism and selfishness is without question; but many commentators do not notice the obvious fact that these treaties were not the cause of the European War; they were negotiated after the war had already commenced. This holds true at least for the Allied powers which went to war in 1914. No spoils treaty antedated the war. In the cases of Italy and Roumania, the secret treaties by which they entered the conflict represented what the Allies had to promise to them in advance in order to bring them over.

There were five of these treaties or understandings, or groups of such, made to solidify the enthusiasm of the original Allies and to bring new ones into the circle.

(1) Russia secured her claims by a treaty with Great Britain and France made in March, 1915, at the beginning of the Allied attack on the Dardanelles. By this the two western Allies agreed that Russia might annex Constantinople and the Asiatic shore of the Bosporus and the Dardanelles, leaving free transit of the straits for the merchant ships of all nations. Russia on her part agreed to the separation of the Caliphate from Turkey and to sharing with France and Great Britain an influence over other portions of the Turkish Empire, reserving to England particular influence in the neighborhood of the Suez Canal and the Gulf of Persia—the British buffer of influence in Persia also was to be extended. These partitions of the Turkish Empire were marked out with more precision—conformable to the later mandates to France and Great Britain—in supplementary understandings (the Sykes-Picot agreement of May 16, 1916, and the agreement at St. Jean de Maurienne, April 17, 1917), reserving for Italy (in conformance with the Treaty of London) a share in the region of Adalia (which the entrance of Greece into the war later stopped her from taking, after the European peace). Thus did the Allies imperturbably dispose of the territory of Germany's Turkish ally, that vigorous "sick man of Europe" near whose bedside the European powers for a century had been waiting either so anxiously or so eagerly.

(2) Italy's claim to expansion had been recognized in principle by the Treaty of London (April 26, 1915) which brought, or bought, that nation into the war. The Central Powers had been willing to promise a redemption of Italy's irredentist population at the end of the war, but not to deliver immediate occupation of the territory concerned. Ardent to weaken their enemy, the Allies promised the irredentist territory with strategical control of the Adriatic and of the Alpine passage into Austria, specifying a line which delivered over to Italy a Slavic and an Austrian irredentum at the head of the Adriatic and on its eastern shores.

Italy was also to have the strategic part of Albania, unchallenged government of the Dodecanese Islands in the Eastern Mediterranean, and a share in the partition of the Turkish Empire.

(3) Roumania was in a most favorable position for bargaining: the Central Powers offered her the irredentist province of Bessarabia, Russian; but the Entente Allies offered her the larger and more populous irredentist part of Hungarian Transylvania and even the Banat of Temesvar, where there was a numerous Serb population. After much wavering Roumania accepted the Allies' offer (Treaty of Bucharest, August 8, 1916), and entered on their side, only to be speedily crushed and occupied during the remainder of the war by German, Austro-Hungarian, and Bulgarian troops. Her separate treaty of peace in 1918 abrogated the obligations of the Allies.

(4) In the Far East, Japan and Great Britain by mutual understanding had divided up the conquered German islands in the Pacific: at the outset of the war British forces occupied those islands south of the Equator; Japan took over those north of that line. When it became apparent that the United States might enter the war Japan reached an understanding (February–March, 1917) with Great Britain, France, Italy and Russia, sanctioning her claim to the transfer of all German right in the Chinese province of Shantung, and, of course, to the islands north of the Equator.

(5) Finally there was the arrangement between France and Russia, also made (March 11, 1917) after the United States had broken relations with Germany, just on the eve of the first Russian Revolution. Each gave the other a free hand in arranging its frontier on the side of Germany—this meant at least Alsace-Lorraine for France and the Polish provinces for Russia.

Such were the famous secret agreements which Arthur Balfour presumably had in his portfolio, with their boundaries drawn on a large map, when he hurried to Washington in April, 1917, to secure full American participation in the war on the continent of Europe. To his surprise he found the United States enthusiastic for winning the war first and talking peace only afterward. Congress was appropriating (April 24, 1917) $7,000,000,000 of which $3,000,000,000 was to be loaned to Allied governments, the first great credit of a total which rapidly mounted to $7,077,144,750 before the armistice of November 11, 1918, and $2,170,200,000 more after it.

The President felt it would be a pity to let Balfour go home without a thorough discussion of the peace terms of the Allies. Colonel House thought it would be inadvisable at that time to have a general discussion with all the Allies: "If the Allies begin to discuss terms among themselves," he wrote to the President, "they will soon hate one another worse than they do Germany and a situation will arise similar to that in the Balkan States after the Turkish War. It seems to me that the only thing to be considered at present is how to beat Germany in the quickest way." Balfour easily concurred in House's sentiments. During the Balfour mission peace terms were nevertheless canvassed in long conferences. To Colonel House Balfour showed his map with the territorial lines of the secret treaties drawn on it. With the President and House, he went over the same ground. Russia had now collapsed, and the British spokesman did not defend her claims in Washington: Constantinople might be a free city, and Poland a resurrected state,

upon the seas, outside territorial waters, alike in peace and in war, except as the seas may be closed in whole or in part by international action for the enforcement of international covenant.

3. The removal, so far as possible, of all economic barriers and the establishment of an equality of trade conditions among all the nations consenting to the peace and associating themselves for its maintenance.

4. Adequate guaranties given and taken that national armaments will be reduced to the lowest point consistent with domestic safety.

5. A free, open-minded, and absolutely impartial adjustment of all colonial claims, based upon a strict observance of the principle that in determining all such questions of sovereignty the interests of the populations concerned *must* have equal weight with the equitable claims of the government whose title is to be determined.

6. The evacuation of all Russian territory and such a settlement of all questions affecting Russia as will secure the best and freest co-operation of the other nations of the world in obtaining for her an unhampered and unembarrassed opportunity for the independent determination of her own political development and national policy and assure her of a sincere welcome into the society of free nations under institutions of her own choosing; and, more than a welcome, assistance also of every kind that she may need and may herself desire. The treatment accorded Russia by her sister nations in the months to come will be the acid test of their good will, of their comprehension of her needs as distinguished from their own interests, and of their intelligent and unselfish sympathy.

7. Belgium, the whole world will agree, *must* be evacuated and restored,

without any attempt to limit the sovereignty which she enjoys in common with all other free nations. No other single act will serve as this will serve to restore confidence among the nations in the laws which they have themselves set and determined for the government of their relations with one another. Without this healing act the whole structure and validity of international law is forever impaired.

8. All French territory *should* be freed and the invaded portions restored, and the wrong done to France by Prussia in 1871 in the matter of Alsace-Lorraine, which has unsettled the peace of the world for nearly fifty years, *should* be righted, in order that peace may once more be made secure in the interest of all.

9. A readjustment of the frontiers of Italy *should* be effected along clearly recognizable lines of nationality.

10. The peoples of Austria-Hungary, whose place among the nations we wish to see safeguarded and assured, *should* be accorded the freest opportunity of autonomous development.

11. Roumania, Serbia, and Montenegro *should* be evacuated; occupied territories restored; Serbia accorded free and secure access to the sea; and the relations of the several Balkan states to one another determined by friendly counsel along historically established lines of allegiance and nationality; and international guaranties of the political and economic independence and territorial integrity of the several Balkan states *should* be entered into.

12. The Turkish portions of the present Ottoman Empire *should* be assured a secure sovereignty, but the other nationalities which are now under Turkish rule *should* be assured an undoubted security of life and an absolutely unmo-

lested opportunity of autonomous development, and the Dardanelles *should* be permanently opened as a free passage to the ships and commerce of all nations under international guaranties.

13. An independent Polish state *should* be erected, which *should* include the territories inhabited by indisputably Polish populations, which *should* be assured a free and secure access to the sea, and whose political and economic independence and territorial integrity *should* be guarantied by international covenant.

14. A general association of nations *must* be formed under specific covenants for the purpose of affording mutual guaranties of political independence and territorial integrity to great and small states alike."

The President and Colonel House studiously went over the whole document after they had first drafted it, qualifying it with their *musts* and *shoulds*.

The Fourteen Points, it proved, were to be interpreted under conditions of complete victory and solely by the Allied and Associated Powers, with the defeated enemy reaching desperately to the Wilsonian principles in the hope to save at least something. In these circumstances it was easy for the victors to interpret *should* to mean *must*.

The final German offensive in the west failed in July, 1918. The Turkish, Bulgarian and Austrian allies began to crack all along their respective fronts and at home. With the victory now surely in sight, the Allies themselves were reeling with exhaustion. During 1918 there took place a series of long-distance exchanges of peace views in the shape of pronouncements from the rostrums of the different governments. These varied in their force according to the military situation. At no time were the Allies driven

to accepting a "peace by compromise and negotiation" which the Central Powers offered. Meanwhile President Wilson in public addresses had piled the Fourteen Points with further general principles of durable peace which included: the destruction or at least reduction of arbitrary power capable of upsetting the peace of the world, satisfaction of "well-defined national aspirations," prohibition of especial leagues or embargoes within the proposed League of Nations, no secret treaties, self-determination for peoples and territories whose sovereignty was in question, and, finally, "impartial justice."

The end of the war suddenly appeared when Bulgaria signed an armistice of military surrender and occupation, September 29, 1918. Already Austria-Hungary (September 16, 1918) had proposed to the enemy a discussion of peace by all belligerents. Facing complete collapse, and in panic at the furious and general advance of the Allies and Associates all along the western front, General Ludendorff and the Field Marshal von Hindenburg, the German Chief of Staff, urgently advised the Government to sue for peace and to try to salvage something by an appeal to the Wilsonian principles. On October 6, Germany, and on October 7, Austria-Hungary, transmitted to the United States (instead of to the Allies) a request for an armistice. With victorious troops exultantly pushing through on all fronts the President made the most of his advantage, and kept control of the preliminary moves for peace. He used in a masterly way the strategy of delay. In a correspondence with Germany he insisted that he must know that he was treating with a government that really had the support of the people; to Austria he replied that the recent recognition of the belligerency of Czechoslo-

invoked a partisan issue where previously there had been little for the public to discern between the two parties united in war. The country was normally Republican—Wilson had come to power and stayed in power only because of the division of his Republican opponents; now, with the war over, they united to meet his challenge.

The elections resulted in a clear Republican majority for the new Senate (and House too) which would meet after March 4, 1919, to consider the treaties of peace. Ex-President Roosevelt, presuming to speak for a reunited and victorious Republican Party, declared to the world after the election: "Our allies and our enemies, and Mr. Wilson himself, should all understand that Mr. Wilson has no authority whatever to speak for the American people at this time. His leadership has just been emphatically repudiated by them. . . ."

The world cried for peace. The overturn of three great empires, Germany, Austria-Hungary, and Russia, and their satellites, displayed throughout the eastern half of Europe a panorama of confusion, anarchy and chaos. The question of the hour was how to shape the machinery of procedure directly, and efficaciously, to dictate peace quickly on the terms of the Allied and Associated Powers, terms couched as yet in the very general Wilsonian principles. France had suggested to the United States, in a memorandum to Washington of November 29, 1918, that the five great victors (the United States, Great Britain, France, Italy, Japan) should sweep the table clear of all previous special agreements arrived at by some of the Allies only, and straightway agree among themselves on the principal bases of peace. The small belligerents, the neutral states, and the new states in forma-

tion could be called in for consultation as their special interests were touched on one by one. In subsequent conferences, after a preliminary peace had been dictated, garnished with the invocation of moral principles, all the nations could meet in a congress to work out the permanent organization of world peace in a League of Nations. Colonel House and Secretary Lansing were inclined to favor some such procedure. President Wilson did not even answer the French proposal. He had his mind first on a League of Nations. He was determined that it should be interwoven with the peace treaties, and that he himself would take the American delegation to Paris to make sure that this was done; otherwise the peoples of the embattled nations might be overreached by the more sophisticated spokesmen of their governments. He did not realize that actually the peoples could be more uncompromising than their spokesmen.

If repudiated by the electorate of his own homeland, it was at the apogee of his prestige in the world that Woodrow Wilson surveyed the European shore from the bridge of the *George Washington*. He arrived in Europe as a true friend of mankind, closer to the principles of Christian charity and justice than any statesman in history. The new great ideal seemed really possible. If only he could bring Europe to agree to a peace of justice resting on the foundations of a league of democratic nations which would execute and regulate the treaties of peace, he was convinced that the opposition of Congress at home would have to yield to the force of public opinion. By the gospel of his principles he would overbear the Republican politicians in the Senate, as abroad he expected to sweep aside whatever obstacles the Allies' secret treaties presented to the application of his Fourteen Points.

The American Peace Commission consisted of executive agents appointed without the advice and consent of the Senate, a custom which had been engrafted by practice to the American constitutional system by virtue of the President's control over diplomatic negotiations. In the language of the treaties which he later signed, the President was "acting in his own name and by his own proper authority." Very unwisely he did not include in the Commission, according to traditional practice, representatives from both parties in that Senate which would be called upon to ratify his treaties. He was also criticized, even by his own Secretary of State, for jeopardizing his dominant position in the world by descending into a conference with the foreign statesmen in Europe. One of the real advantages of the American diplomatic system has been the reserve power which the President, back home across the ocean, has had to stiffen the demands of his plenipotentiaries in the give and take of negotiation; and back of this, and despite the shocking abuse of it by party politics, lies the still greater reserve power of the Senate in the right to advise and consent, by a two-thirds majority, to the ratification of any treaty. These advantages the President, in his convictions, threw away by going to Paris at the head of a personal executive delegation. The other members were: Secretary of State Robert Lansing; Colonel Edward M. House, the President's constant political mentor; General Tasker H. Bliss; and Mr. Henry White, veteran career diplomatist of pale Republican allegiance, who had never made any public statement hostile to the President. The latter was the only Republican on the Commission, and through him Senator Lodge, leader of the Republican Senate and chairman of the Committee on Foreign Relations, unsuccessfully tried to speak to the Allies behind the back of the President.

A shipload of officials of the State Department, intelligence officers, specialists and secretaries accompanied the Commission. The "experts" had been recruited quietly from academic and other walks of life under the direction of Colonel House. Organized unostentatiously under the name of The Inquiry, after the immemorial habit of professors everywhere, they had diligently assembled during the previous twelve months a mass of facts and information of a special nature for the advice of the diplomatists who were to discuss the intricate political, territorial and economic questions of several continents. These specialists played an important part in drafting the non-debatable articles of the peace treaties and in fortifying the plenipotentiaries in the diplomatic disputations.

At the Peace Conference at Paris, which opened January 12, 1919, met the plenipotentiaries of twenty-seven nations, enemies of Germany or of her allies, or nations, like five of the Latin-American states, who had severed relations with Germany. There had never been such a diplomatic gathering in history. Even the Congress of Vienna, once consecrated to the principle of Nationality, could not approach its vast importance. It was the focus of seething national rivalries, resentments, despairs, ambitions, triumphs. President Wilson, it must be generally conceded, was the only statesman of the great powers who had no selfish national interest to serve, no particular necessitous war bargain to fulfill. Each of the other war-weary nations, except for those like the South

mandatory under the direction of the League of Nations, in each instance, proved to be either the conqueror or the beneficiary of a secret treaty. Men have sneered at this as a hypocritical disguise of annexation; at least it was an appeal to an international control of backward peoples and colonial areas, stakes of imperialistic contention. The efficacy of the system would depend on the strength of the League of Nations.

France required a demilitarized buffer Rhineland state to protect her from dreaded German attacks in the future; and she insisted on repayment of separation allowances and military pensions to civilian relatives and survivors of soldiers. Here were the most difficult issues. They were settled by France agreeing to content herself with Alsace-Lorraine and her old frontiers, back of a military occupation for fifteen years of the left bank of the Rhine and its bridgeheads, and a demilitarized zone in Germany for a depth of 50 kilometers east of the Rhine; in return France was to possess the Saar Valley, with its rich coal mines, subject to a determining plebiscite in 1935 (as a result of which the district was finally returned to Germany). Clemenceau, against the advice of Marshal Foch, agreed to this only when Lloyd George and Wilson signed a tripartite alliance pledging their countries to come to the aid of France if attacked in the future by Germany. It was strictly and significantly stated that the alliance would not apply unless ratified by all three parties, according to their respective constitutional requirements. Great Britain and France ratified. The United States Senate, as President Wilson probably knew it would and as Premier Clemenceau must have suspected it would, refused to consider the pro-

posed pact, so radically contrary to George Washington's historic advice against "permanent alliances." The President made no great battle for this treaty in the Senate. It was a way the diplomatists had to get around a difficult corner. The President and the Prime Minister readily agreed to Clemenceau's demand that the dubious allowances for military separation and pensions be added to the German debt of reparations under category of "civilian damages" sanctioned by the Armistice. Computations of this kind could double the already astronomical character of calculating reparations debits—projecting their reckoning even unto the outer spaces of the ether drift beyond the great Magellanic Cloud.

In the case of Italy, the President assented to the strategical frontier of the Treaty of London, with some modifications, but not including the city of Fiume. The treaty of peace with Austria gave Italy possession of the Alpine passes into Austria, creating an Austria *irredenta* in the Tyrol of some 250,000 souls, in place of the old *Italia irredenta*. It remained to fix the boundary between Italy and the new state of Jugoslavia at the head of the Adriatic and along the Dalmatian littoral. President Wilson sought to apply Point 9 of the Fourteen Points to temper the extreme Italian claims, but it is uncertain whether Italy was explicitly bound by the Fourteen Points in the armistice with Austria-Hungary. Wilson, Lloyd George and Clemenceau were willing to make generous strategic concessions to Italy beyond the line of the Treaty of London, but not to give to Italy the half-Slavic city of Fiume, necessary for a usable outlet for Jugoslavia to the sea, a city of mixed population with an entirely Slavic hinterland. The peace conference ended without this intricate question being settled.

Japan insisted on two things, an explicit recognition in the Covenant of the League of Nations of the principle of equality of all races, and title to her conquests from Germany in the Chinese province of Shantung as well as control of the conquered former German islands north of the Equator. She was willing to accept a mandate for the islands, a mandate of the class which administered them as integral parts of the mandatory state, except for prohibiting fortification; and she even made the promise ultimately to get out of Shantung in her own way, a promise subsequently fulfilled. Unfortunately the Council did not agree to the principle of racial equality. If also it had refused to transfer to Japan the German holdings in Shantung, Japan undoubtedly would have left the Conference and refused the treaty; with European powers still on the mainland of Asia, she was determined not to have dictated to her, after 1895, another relinquishment of the fruits of victory. To secure Japanese assent to the treaty and hence to the League, President Wilson reluctantly accepted the Japanese position in Shantung, contrary as it was to the gospel of self-determination. China then refused to sign the Treaty of Versailles, but became a member of the League of Nations by ratifying the Treaty of St. Germain with Austria, which cost her none of her own territory, though it also violated in Central Europe the consecrated principles of self-determination and nationality.

All these major concessions in principle the President made in order to secure the consent of all the great victor powers to the League of Nations as an integral part of the treaty. He believed that the regrettable compromises in each case justified the great end in view.

The other provisions of the treaties with Germany, Austria, and Hungary involved no essential difficulty, although there was intense disputation in regard to the regulation of the status of the Saar Valley before the plebiscite postponed until 1935, and concerning the establishment of the Free City of Danzig at the mouth of the Polish Corridor. They contained, among the countless routine articles: creation of the special commission to calculate and to charge up to Germany the total sum due for reparations, with no indemnity for war expenses by the Allies; the shaping of the nine new remnant and succession states in Central Europe—Austria, Hungary, Czechoslovakia, Jugoslavia, Poland, Lithuania, Latvia, Estonia, Finland; the Polish Corridor; the marking off of patches of German peripheral territory for determination of sovereignty by plebiscites; the regulation of the Kiel Canal and the rivers within enemy territory; the effectual disarmament of Germany and her allies on land, on sea, and in the air "in order to render possible the initiation of a general limitation of the armaments of all nations"; and the one hundred and one incidental details of so vast a settlement of peace. The Principal Allied and Associated Powers were easily agreed on the famous Article 231 and its sweeping provisions: "The Allied and Associated Governments affirm and Germany accepts the responsibility of Germany and her allies for causing all the loss and damage to which the Allied and Associated Governments and their nationals have been subjected as a consequence of the war imposed upon them by the aggression of Germany and her allies."

Strictly speaking, this article required

and our Allies, in boastful and unseemly language, to a level of morality and of international disinterestedness which, whatever the faults of others, we can not claim. But above all, should not the future peace of the world have been our highest and guiding motive? Men of all nations had suffered together, the victims of a curse deep-seated in the past history and present weakness of the European race. The lifting of the curse was a better object in the treaty, if universal justice were our aim, than its relentless execution.

Its Honorableness

But there was another aspect of justice, more earthly perhaps than the high topics which have just occupied us—the question of our promises, in reliance on which the enemy had capitulated. Beginning with the invasion of Belgium, the Allied countries had pronounced the sacredness of engagements and the maintenance of international good faith as among their principal objects. Only thus, in the judgment of the considered wisdom of the world, only by the establishment of the rule of law as between nations, can national egotisms be tempered and the stability of settlements be preserved. It was therefore peculiarly incumbent upon us to practise what we had preached, and even to be so scrupulous as not to take advantage of an ambiguous phrase.

To understand the peace, therefore, and its effect on general confidence in the fairness of the Allies, we have to remember the history of the negotiations which began with the German note of October 5, 1918, and concluded with President Wilson's note of November 5, 1918.

*   *   *

The Armistice Contract

The nature of the contract between Germany and the Allies resulting from this exchange of documents is plain and unequivocal. The terms of the peace are to be in accordance with the addresses of the President, and the purpose of the Peace Conference is "to discuss the details of their application." The circumstances of the contract were of an unusually solemn and binding character; for one of the conditions of it was that Germany should agree to armistice terms which were to be such as would leave her helpless.

What, then, was the substance of this contract to which the Allies had bound themselves? I have examined this in detail in my book. In a word, we were committed to a peace based upon the Fourteen Points and upon the principle that "there shall be no annexations, no contributions, no punitive damages."

It is still maintained by some persons that the enemy surrendered unconditionally and that we are in no way bound by the engagements outlined above. This has been maintained lately, for example, in a lengthy article contributed to the New York *Times* by General Greene. Other advocates of the treaty stand upon the other leg and maintain that, while we are bound by the Fourteen Points, the peace treaty is in substantial conformity with them. This, I understand, is the attitude of President Wilson. I am reckoned a hostile critic of the President because I believe that he holds this attitude sincerely, having been partly deceived and partly self-deceived, his thought and feeling being here cast in what, for lack of a more descriptive phrase, I termed a theological mold. His friends argue, however, that he was well aware of what he was doing in Paris and deliberately sacrificed some part of his professions in the interests of the higher political expediency.

*   *   *

But there remains the question—greater than that of the actions and motives of individuals—whether in fact we have kept faith with our enemies. I have maintained that on certain matters we have not kept faith, the most important instance within the economic sphere, which was my particular subject-matter, being the inclusion in our reparation claims of huge sums for military pensions and separation allowances, which greatly swell the bill and to which we are not entitled. Our treatment of the Saar Valley, of tariffs and of Germany's river system affords other examples.

Let me here limit myself to the reparation claims. I venture to assert that my criticism of these claims has not been seriously controverted by anyone. It has been stated, since my book appeared, that the President's own advisers in Paris informed him that these claims were illegitimate. Many critics have passed over in silence this particular issue. Yet if it is in fact the case that we have not kept our engagements, is it not a matter of some importance to the national honor of each one of the Allied and Associated countries, and to the moral government of the world?

Those who have defended the treaty on this issue have done so on the most extraordinary grounds. I select below some of the commoner lines of argument. Some say that Germany, if she had won, would not have kept faith with us, and that this fact absolves us from being overscrupulous with her; the enemy, being themselves unjust—this argument asserts—are not entitled to better treatment in return.

Others say that the information we now have makes it probable that Germany could have been compelled to surrender unconditionally, and that for this reason the President's *pourparlers* before the armistice lose much of their binding character.

Others point out that our engagements were in part vaguely expressed; that they were not cast in a legal form; that there is no one to enforce them; and that they can not therefore constitute a "contract." (Imagine, however, with what indignation these same apologists would explode before a similar argument on the lips of a German.)

Others, again, discover that the President was exceeding his powers in his preliminary negotiations as to the basis of the peace, in reliance on which the enemy laid down his arms; and that his promises consequently bound no one.

These are all of them types of man's eternal reasons for not keeping his promises, and their roots are in human nature. But they ill accord with the victorious issue of a crusade for the sanctity of international engagements.

THE TREATY'S WISDOM

With these brief comments I pass from the justice of the treaty, which can not be ignored even when it is not our central topic, to its wisdom and its expediency. Under these heads my criticism of the treaty is double. In the first place, this treaty ignores the economic solidarity of Europe, and by aiming at the destruction of the economic life of Germany it threatens the health and prosperity of the Allies themselves. In the second place, by making demands the execution of which is in the literal sense impossible, it stultifies itself and leaves

Europe more unsettled than it found it. The treaty, by overstepping the limits of the possible, has in practice settled nothing. The true settlement still remains to be made out of the ashes of the present and the disillusionment of the future, when the imposture of Paris is recognized for what it is.

For reasons of historical experience, which are easily understood, and with which all men must sympathize (however profoundly we believe that France will deal to herself as well as to her enemy a fatal wound if she yields to them), there were powerful influences in Paris demanding for the future security of France that the peace should complete the destruction of the economic life of Central Europe, which the war had gone far to consummate.

The Shattered Heart of Europe

The German economic system as it existed before the war depended on three main factors:

1. Overseas commerce, as represented by her mercantile marine, her colonies, her foreign investments, her exports, and the overseas connections of her merchants.

2. The exploitation of her coal and iron and the industries built upon them.

3. Her transport and tariff system.

Of these the first, while not the least important, was certainly the most vulnerable. The treaty aims at the systematic destruction of all three, but principally the first two.

Germany has ceded to the Allies all the vessels of her mercantile marine exceeding sixteen hundred tons gross, half the vessels between one thousand tons and sixteen hundred tons, and one-quarter of her trawlers and other fishing boats. The cession is comprehensive, including not only vessels flying the German flag, but also all vessels owned by Germans but flying other flags, and all vessels under construction as well as those afloat. Further, Germany undertakes, if required, to build for the Allies such types of ships as they may specify, up to two hundred thousand tons annually for five years, the value of these ships being credited to Germany against what is due from her for reparations. Thus the German mercantile marine is swept from the seas and can not be restored for many years to come on a scale adequate to meet the requirements of her own commerce.

Germany has ceded to the Allies "all her rights and titles over her overseas possessions." This cession not only applies to sovereignty but extends on unfavorable terms to government property, all of which, including railways, must be surrendered without payment. Further, in distinction from the practice ruling in the case of most similar cessions in recent history, the property and persons of private German nationals, as distinct from their Government, are also injuriously affected. Not only are German sovereignty and German influence extirpated from the whole of her former overseas possessions, but the persons and property of her nationals resident or owning property in those parts are deprived of legal status and legal security.

The provisions just outlined in regard to the private property of Germans in the ex-German colonies apply equally to private German property in Alsace-Lorraine, except in so far as the French Government may choose to grant exceptions.

The expropriation of German private property is not limited, however, to the ex-German colonies and Alsace-Lorraine. The cumulative effect of a series of complicated provisions, which I have examined in detail in my book, is to deprive Germany (or rather to empower the Allies so to deprive her at their will —it is not yet accomplished) of everything she possesses outside her own frontiers as laid down in the treaty. Not only are her overseas investments taken and her connections destroyed, but the same process of extirpation is applied in the territories of her former allies and of her immediate neighbors by land.

The above provisions relate to Germany's external wealth. Those relating to coal and iron are more important in respect of their ultimate consequences to Germany's internal industrial economy than for the money value immediately involved. The German Empire has been built more truly on coal and iron than on blood and iron. The skilled exploitation of the great coalfields of the Ruhr, Upper Silesia and the Saar alone made possible the development of the steel, chemical and electrical industries which established her as the first industrial nation of continental Europe. One-third of Germany's population lives in towns of more than twenty thousand inhabitants, an industrial concentration which is only possible on a foundation of coal and iron. In striking, therefore, at her coal supply, those who sought her economic destruction were not mistaking their target.

COAL

The coal clauses of the treaty are, however, among those which are likely, by reason of the technical impossibility of their execution, to defeat their own object. If the plebiscite results in Germany's losing the coal districts of Upper Silesia, the treaty will have deprived her of territory from which not far short of one-third of her total coal supply was previously derived. Out of the coal that

remains to her Germany is required, quite rightly, to make good for ten years the estimated loss which France has incurred by the destruction and damage of war in the coalfields of her northern provinces, such deliveries not to exceed twenty million tons in each of the first five years or eight million tons annually thereafter. She has also, over and above this, for ten years to deliver annually seven million tons to France, eight million tons to Belgium, and from four million five hundred thousand tons to eight million five hundred thousand tons to Italy.

I have estimated that this would leave Germany with about sixty million tons annually against domestic requirements, which, on the prewar basis of industry in her remaining territory, would amount to one hundred and ten million tons. In short, Germany could only execute the coal demands of the treaty by abandoning the bulk of her industries and returning to the status of an agricultural country. In this case many millions of her present population could obtain neither work nor food (nor, indeed, facilities of emigration). Yet it is not to be supposed that the population of any country will submit year after year to an export which dooms many of them to starvation and even to death. The thing is humanly and politically impossible. Men will not die so obediently to the dictates of a document. The coal clauses of the treaty are not being executed and never will be.

But in this event the treaty settles nothing, and the extent of the coal deliveries remains as a source of perpetual friction, uncertainty and inefficiency, which will inhibit the industrial activity of all the European countries alike which are parties to it. The coal will not be delivered; it may not even be mined.

No plans which look ahead can be made by anyone. The commodity will be the subject of a perpetual scramble; and even of military occupations and of bloodshed. For, as the result of many various causes, the coal position of all Europe is nearly desperate, and no country will lightly surrender its treaty rights. I affirm, therefore, that the coal clauses are inexpedient and disastrous, and full of danger not only for the economic efficiency but for the political peace of the European continent.

IRON

The provisions relating to iron ore require less detailed attention, though their effects are destructive. They require less attention, because they are in large measure inevitable. Almost exactly seventy-five per cent. of the iron ore raised in Germany in 1913 came from Alsace-Lorraine. But while Lorraine contained seventy-five per cent. of Germany's iron ore, only twenty-five per cent. of her blast-furnaces and of her foundries lay within Lorraine and the Saar basin together, a large proportion of the ore being carried into Germany proper. Thus here, as elsewhere, political considerations cut disastrously across economic.

In a régime of free trade and free economic intercourse it would be of little consequence that iron lay on one side of a political frontier and labor, coal and blast-furnaces on the other. But it seems certain, calculating on the present passions and impulses of European capitalistic society, that the effective iron output of Europe will be diminished by a new political frontier (which sentiment and historic justice require), because nationalism and private interest are thus allowed to impose a new economic frontier along the same lines. These latter

considerations are allowed, in the present governance of Europe, to prevail over the intense need of the continent for the most sustained and efficient production to repair the destruction of war and to satisfy the insistence of labor for a larger reward.

Thus in its coal and iron clauses the treaty strikes at organization and by the destruction of organization impairs yet further the reduced wealth of the whole community.

There remain those treaty provisions which relate to the transport and the tariff systems of Germany. These parts of the treaty have not nearly the importance and significance of those discussed hitherto. They are pin-pricks, interferences and vexations, not so much objectionable for their solid consequences as dishonorable to the Allies in the light of their professions. I can not spare space in this brief article to consider them in the detail they deserve. Taken in their entirety, the economic clauses of the treaty are comprehensive, and little has been overlooked which might impoverish Germany now or obstruct her development in future. So situated, Germany is to make payments of money, on a scale and in a manner about to be examined.

The treaty's claims for an indemnity may be divided into two parts: those which, in accordance with our pre-armistice engagements, we were entitled to make if we judged it expedient to do so, and those which, in my judgment, we had no right to make. The first category includes as its chief items all the direct damages to civilian life and property for which Germany was responsible, more particularly in the invaded and occupied areas of France, Belgium and Serbia, by air-raids, and by the warfare of submarines. It includes also compensation for the improper treatment of interned civilians and for the loot of food, raw materials, live stock, machinery, household effects, timber and the like; and the repayment of fines and requisitions levied on the towns of France and Belgium. I have ventured as a very rough estimate to calculate the total of these items at the following figures:

Belgium	$ 2,500,000,000
France	4,000,000,000
Great Britain . . .	2,850,000,000
Other Allies	1,250,000,000
	$10,600,000,000

I need not impress on the reader that there is much guesswork in the above, and the figure for France in particular has been criticised on the ground that it is too low.

But I feel some confidence that the general magnitude, as distinct from the precise figures, is not very erroneous; and this may be expressed by the statement that a claim against Germany, based on the interpretation of the pre-armistice engagements of the Allied Powers which is adopted above, would assuredly be found to exceed eight billion and to fall short of fifteen billion.

INDEMNITY DEMANDS

This is the amount of the claim which we were entitled to present to the enemy. I believe that it would have been a wise and just act to have asked the German Government at the peace negotiations to agree to a sum of ten billion in final settlement, without further examination of particulars. This would have provided an immediate and certain solution, and would have required from Germany a sum which, if she were granted certain indulgences, it might not have proved entirely impossible for her to pay. This sum should have been divided up among the Allies themselves on a basis of need and general equity.

But the question was not settled on its merits, and the above figure is far from representing the whole of our actual claims under the treaty. As a compromise between keeping the letter of our engagements and demanding the entire cost of the war, which French and British politicians had promised to their constituents from the platform, Paris decided to include a claim, which seemed plausible in itself, which recommended itself to sentiment, and which amounted to a large sum; and Germany has been required to discharge in their entirety all military pensions and separation allowances paid or to be paid, which have arisen out of the war. I have estimated that this adds to the bill an aggregate sum of twenty-five billion dollars made up as follows:

France	$12,000,000,000
British Empire . . .	7,000,000,000
Italy	2,500,000,000
Others (including the United States) . .	3,500,000,000
	$25,000,000,000

Adding this figure to my maximum estimate of fifteen billion dollars, we have a total claim against Germany of about forty billion dollars. While the details making up this total have been criticised and much higher figures have been mentioned (as, for example, seventy-five billion dollars by M. Klotz, then finance minister of France), the world has, generally speaking, accepted my figure as representing the facts as nearly as is at present possible, and as supplying a reasonable basis of discussion.

THE BLANK CHECK

The reader will observe that this figure is mine, and that no final amount is specified by the treaty itself, which fixes no definite sum as representing Germany's liability. This feature has been the subject of very general criticism, that it is equally inconvenient to Germany and to the Allies themselves that she should not know what she has to pay or they what they are to receive. The method, apparently contemplated by the treaty, of arriving at the final result over a period of many months by an addition of hundreds of thousands of individual claims for damage to land, farm buildings and chickens, is evidently impracticable, and the reasonable course would have been for both parties to compound for a round sum without examination of details. If this round sum had been named in the treaty, the settlement would have been placed on a more businesslike basis.

But this was impossible for two reasons. Two different kinds of false statements had been widely promulgated, one as to Germany's capacity to pay, the other as to the amount of the Allies' just claims in respect of the devastated areas. The fixing of either of these figures presented a dilemma. A figure for Germany's prospective capacity to pay, not too much in excess of the estimates of most candid and well-informed authorities, would have fallen hopelessly far short of popular expectations both in England and in France. On the other hand, a definite figure for damage done which would not disastrously disappoint the expectations that had been raised in France and Belgium might have been incapable of substantiation under challenge.

By far the safest course for the politicians was, therefore, to mention no figure at all; and from this necessity a great deal of the complication of the reparation scheme essentially springs.

According to the letter of the treaty, any part of the sum eventually determined as due which remains unpaid from time to time is to accumulate at interest at five per cent. . . . As from May 1, 1921, the capital sum of indebtedness is rolling up all the time at compound interest. The effect of this provision toward increasing the burden is enormous, on the assumption that Germany can not pay very large sums at first. . . .

AN AVALANCHE OF DEBT

That is to say, even if Germany pays seven hundred and fifty million dollars annually up to 1936, she will nevertheless owe us at that date more than half as much again as she does now (sixty-five billion dollars as compared with forty billion dollars). From 1936 onward she will have to pay to us three billion two hundred and fifty million dollars annually in order to keep pace with the interest alone. At the end of any year in which she pays less than this sum she will owe more than she did at the beginning of it. And if she is to discharge the capital sum in thirty years from 1936, i.e., in forty-eight years from the armistice, she must pay an additional six hundred and fifty million dollars annually, making three billion nine hundred million dollars in all.

It is, in my judgment, as certain as anything can be, for reasons which I will summarize in a moment, that Germany can not pay anything approaching this sum. Until the treaty is altered, therefore, Germany has in effect engaged herself to hand over to the Allies the whole of her surplus production in perpetuity.

This is not less the case because the Reparation Commission has been given discretionary powers to vary the rate of interest, and to postpone and even to cancel the capital indebtedness. In the first place, some of these powers can only be exercised if the commission or the governments represented on it are *unanimous*. But also, which is perhaps more important, it will be the *duty* of the Reparation Commission, until there has been a unanimous and far-reaching change of the policy which the treaty represents, to extract from Germany year after year the maximum sum obtainable. There is a great difference between fixing a definite sum, which, though large, is within Germany's capacity to pay and yet to retain a little for herself, and fixing a sum far beyond her capacity, which is then to be reduced at the discretion of a foreign commission, acting with the object of obtaining each year the maximum which the circumstances of that year permit. For the first still leaves her with some slight incentive for enterprise, energy and hope.

GERMANY'S CAPACITY TO PAY

How is Germany placed, in the situation in which the rest of the treaty leaves her, for discharging a vast obligation?

It is evident that Germany's pre-war capacity to pay an annual foreign tribute has not been unaffected by the almost total loss of her colonies, her overseas connections, her mercantile marine, and her foreign properties; by the cession of ten per cent. of her territory and population, of one-third of her coal and of three-quarters of her iron ore; by two million casualties among men in the prime of life; by the starvation of her people for four years; by the burden of a vast war debt; by the depreciation of her currency to less than one-seventh its former value; by the disruption of her allies and their territories; by revolution at home and Bolshevism on her borders;

and by all the unmeasured ruin in strength and hope of four years of all-swallowing war and final defeat.

All this, one would have supposed, is evident. Yet most estimates of a great indemnity from Germany depend on the assumption that she is in a position to conduct in the future a vastly greater trade than ever she has had in the past.

The forms in which Germany can discharge her debt are three and three only: (1) immediately transferable wealth in the form of gold, ships and foreign securities; (2) the value of property in ceded territory or surrendered under the armistice; and (3) annual payments spread over a term of years, partly in cash and partly in materials such as coal products, potash and dyes. There is no other way whatever. . . .

It is not possible within the limits of the space here at my disposal to enter into the details of this examination. But my broad conclusion is that in the actual facts of the case there is no reasonable probability of Germany's being able to make payments in excess of five hundred million dollars annually. This figure has not been challenged in detail by anyone, and has been supported, as being in the neighborhood of the best estimate, by many distinguished authorities.

HER EXPORT POWERS

Yet an enormously increased export is necessary. For, so far from Germany's exports exceeding her imports before the war, her imports exceeded her exports on the average of the five years ending 1913 by about three hundred and seventy million dollars. On the assumptions, therefore, (1) that we do not specially favor Germany over ourselves in supplies of such raw materials as cotton and wool (the world's supply of which is limited); (2) that France, having secured the iron-ore deposits, makes a serious attempt to secure the blast-furnaces and the steel trade also; (3) that Germany is not encouraged and assisted to undercut the iron and other trades of the Allies in overseas markets; and (4) that a substantial preference is not given to German goods in the British Empire and other Allied countries, it becomes evident by examination of the specific items that not much is practicable.

I reach, therefore, the final conclusion that, including all methods of payment—immediately transferable wealth, ceded property and an annual tribute—ten billion dollars is a safe maximum figure of Germany's capacity to pay. In all the actual circumstances, I do not believe that she can pay as much.

A capacity of forty billion dollars or even of twenty-five billion dollars is, therefore, not within the limits of reasonable possibility. It is for those who believe that Germany can make an annual payment amounting to thousands of millions of dollars to say *in what specific commodities* they intend this payment to be made, and *in what markets* the goods are to be sold. Until they proceed to some degree of detail, and are able to produce some tangible argument in favor of their conclusions, they do not deserve to be believed.

A Dead Treaty

Such, in brief, are the economic provisions of the Treaty of Versailles, which the United States has refused to ratify and most of Europe would now unwrite if it could. A year has passed since it came into existence, and authority has already passed from it—not, in my judgment, because there has been much softening of sentiment toward Germany, but because the treaty is no treaty, because

it is now generally recognized that in truth it settles nothing. After what has passed, Europe requires above all a *settlement*, and this the treaty has not given it. If you pledge a man to perform the impossible, you are no nearer a decision as to what in fact he is to do; for his pledge is, necessarily, a dead letter. The reparation and coal clauses of the treaty are its most important economic features. But being composed of foolish, idle words, having no relation to the real facts, they are without practical effect, and they leave the prospects of the future undetermined.

What, then, are we to do? Before I venture an answer, there is one element in the attitude of the United States to the treaty which deserves attention. The United States has refused to ratify the treaty; the United States gets nothing out of the treaty; the ideals of the vast majority of the inhabitants of the United States are probably at variance with the treaty; even at Paris it was the representatives of the United States who fought most sincerely and resolutely for the modification of the treaty—yet it is in the United States that the treaty now finds its most whole-hearted defenders.

The Situation Here

The explanation of the paradox is to be found, I think, in this: in England the treaty was swallowed in the first instance without much criticism or comment; it has never become in any intense degree a party question; Mr. Lloyd George himself now appears among those most willing to modify it; and consequently there is no vested interest in defending it. But in the United States the treaty has become a bitter party question. The President, in a spirit, as I believe, of sincere delusion, or, as his friends maintain, of calculated wisdom, has maneuvered himself or been maneuvered into the position of defending the integral acceptance of the document. The personal adherents of the President must follow his single track. An American professor or an American lawyer back from the Conference writes about the treaty in newspaper articles of hot eulogy, such as are not common in Europe. My own American colleagues from Paris, whose views I so much shared and whose labors against the treaty I so much admired, now, alas! find themselves committed by loyalty to an honored chief to representing the treaty, what no one in Europe now thinks it, as an instrument of substantial wisdom. Truly the President carries his own cross, doomed by a perverse fate to support a settlement which has at the same time shattered his prestige and defeated his ideals.

It will therefore be difficult, I fear—though I speak at a distance and without knowledge—so long as the treaty remains a party issue, for the United States to approach its great problems in the impartial and disinterested spirit which their special position makes possible and will, I believe, eventually make actual.

* * *

Let me add that I differ profoundly from those who, admitting the imperfections of the treaty, look for succor to the provisions contained in it for its progressive modification in practice by the unanimous consent of the leading Allies. The difference between revising the treaty at once and progressively modifying it under the force of circumstances is the difference between building a firm foundation and underpinning day by day a tottering structure. . . .

John Maynard Keynes: II. WILSON

IT happens, however, that it is not only an ideal question that is at issue. My purpose in this book is to show that the Carthaginian peace is not *practically* right or possible. Although the school of thought from which it springs is aware of the economic factor, it overlooks, nevertheless, the deeper economic tendencies which are to govern the future. The clock cannot be set back. You cannot restore Central Europe to 1870 without setting up such strains in the European structure and letting loose such human and spiritual forces as, pushing beyond frontiers and races, will overwhelm not only you and your "guarantees," but your institutions, and the existing order of your society.

By what legerdemain was this policy substituted for the Fourteen Points, and how did the President come to accept it? The answer to these questions is difficult and depends on elements of character and psychology and on the subtle influence of surroundings, which are hard to detect and harder still to describe. But, if ever the action of a single individual matters, the collapse of the

From *The Economic Consequences of the Peace* (pp. 36–55) by John Maynard Keynes, copyright, 1920, by Harcourt, Brace and Company, Inc.; renewed 1948 by Lydia Lopokova Keynes. Reprinted by permission of Harcourt, Brace and Company, Inc.

President has been one of the decisive
moral events of history; and I must make
an attempt to explain it. What a place
the President held in the hearts and
hopes of the world when he sailed to us
in the *George Washington!* What a great
man came to Europe in those early days
of our victory!

In November, 1918, the armies of
Foch and the words of Wilson had
brought us sudden escape from what
was swallowing up all we cared for. The
conditions seemed favorable beyond any
expectation. The victory was so complete that fear need play no part in the
settlement. The enemy had laid down
his arms in reliance on a solemn compact
as to the general character of the peace,
the terms of which seemed to assure a
settlement of justice and magnanimity
and a fair hope for a restoration of the
broken current of life. To make assurance certain, the President was coming
himself to set the seal on his work.

When President Wilson left Washington he enjoyed a prestige and a moral
influence throughout the world un-
equaled in history. His bold and meas-
ured words carried to the peoples of
Europe above and beyond the voices of
their own politicians. The enemy peoples trusted him to carry out the compact he had made with them; and the
Allied peoples acknowledged him not as
a victor only but almost as a prophet. In
addition to this moral influence the realities of power were in his hands. The
American armies were at the height of
their numbers, discipline, and equipment. Europe was in complete depend-
ence on the food supplies of the United
States; and financially she was even more
absolutely at their mercy. Europe not
only already owed the United States
more than she could pay; but only a
large measure of further assistance could

save her from starvation and bankruptcy.
Never had a philosopher held such
weapons wherewith to bind the princes
of this world. How the crowds of the
European capitals pressed about the carriage of the President! With what curi-
osity, anxiety, and hope we sought a
glimpse of the features and bearing of
the man of destiny who, coming from
the West, was to bring healing to the
wounds of the ancient parent of his
civilization and lay for us the foundations of the future.

The disillusion was so complete that
some of those who had trusted most
hardly dared speak of it. Could it be
true? they asked of those who returned
from Paris. Was the Treaty really as bad
as it seemed? What had happened to
the President? What weakness or what
misfortune had led to so extraordinary,
so unlooked-for a betrayal?

Yet the causes were very ordinary and
human. The President was not a hero
or a prophet; he was not even a philosopher; but a generously intentioned
man, with many of the weaknesses of
other human beings, and lacking that
dominating   intellectual   equipment
which would have been necessary to
cope with the subtle and dangerous
spellbinders whom a tremendous clash
of forces and personalities had brought
to the top as triumphant masters in the
swift game of give and take, face to face
in council—a game of which he had no
experience at all.

We had indeed quite a wrong idea of
the President. We knew him to be solitary and aloof, and believed him very
strong-willed and obstinate. We did not
figure him as a man of detail, but the
clearness with which he had taken hold
of certain main ideas would, we thought,
in combination with his tenacity, enable
him to sweep through cobwebs. Besides

these qualities he would have the objectivity, the cultivation, and the wide knowledge of the student. The great distinction of language which had marked his famous Notes seemed to indicate a man of lofty and powerful imagination. His portraits indicated a fine presence and a commanding delivery. With all this he had attained and held with increasing authority the first position in a country where the arts of the politician are not neglected. All of which, without expecting the impossible, seemed a fine combination of qualities for the matter in hand.

The first impression of Mr. Wilson at close quarters was to impair some but not all of these illusions. His head and features were finely cut and exactly like his photographs, and the muscles of his neck and the carriage of his head were distinguished. But, like Odysseus, the President looked wiser when he was seated; and his hands, though capable and fairly strong, were wanting in sensitiveness and finesse. The first glance at the President suggested not only that, whatever else he might be, his temperament was not primarily that of the student or the scholar, but that he had not much even of that culture of the world which marks M. Clemenceau and Mr. Balfour as exquisitely cultivated gentlemen of their class and generation. But more serious than this, he was not only insensitive to his surroundings in the external sense, he was not sensitive to his environment at all. What chance could such a man have against Mr. Lloyd George's unerring, almost medium-like, sensibility to everyone immediately round him? To see the British Prime Minister watching the company, with six or seven senses not available to ordinary men, judging character, motive, and subconscious impulse, perceiving

what each was thinking and even what each was going to say next, and compounding with telepathic instinct the argument or appeal best suited to the vanity, weakness, or self-interest of his immediate auditor, was to realize that the poor President would be playing blind man's bluff in that party. Never could a man have stepped into the parlor a more perfect and predestined victim to the finished accomplishments of the Prime Minister. The Old World was tough in wickedness anyhow; the Old World's heart of stone might blunt the sharpest blade of the bravest knight-errant. But this blind and deaf Don Quixote was entering a cavern where the swift and glittering blade was in the hands of the adversary.

But if the President was not the philosopher-king, what was he? After all he was a man who had spent much of his life at a university. He was by no means a businessman or an ordinary party politician, but a man of force, personality, and importance. What, then, was his temperament?

The clue once found was illuminating. The President was like a Nonconformist minister, perhaps a Presbyterian. His thought and his temperament were essentially theological, not intellectual, with all the strength and the weakness of that manner of thought, feeling, and expression. It is a type of which there are not now in England and Scotland such magnificent specimens as formerly; but this description, nevertheless, will give the ordinary Englishman the distinctest impression of the President.

With this picture of him in mind, we can return to the actual course of events. The President's program for the world, as set forth in his speeches and his Notes, had displayed a spirit and a purpose so admirable that the last desire of his sympathizers was to criticize details—the details, they felt, were quite rightly not filled in at present, but would be in due course. It was commonly believed at the commencement of the Paris Conference that the President had thought out, with the aid of a large body of advisers, a comprehensive scheme not only for the League of Nations, but for the embodiment of the Fourteen Points in an actual Treaty of Peace. But in fact the President had thought out nothing; when it came to practice his ideas were nebulous and incomplete. He had no plan, no scheme, no constructive ideas whatever for clothing with the flesh of life the commandments which he had thundered from the White House. He could have preached a sermon on any of them or have addressed a stately prayer to the Almighty for their fulfilment; but he could not frame their concrete application to the actual state of Europe.

He not only had no proposals in detail, but he was in many respects, perhaps inevitably, ill-informed as to European conditions. And not only was he ill-informed—that was true of Mr. Lloyd George also—but his mind was slow and unadaptable. The President's slowness amongst the Europeans was noteworthy. He could not, all in a minute, take in what the rest were saying, size up the situation with a glance, frame a reply, and meet the case by a slight change of ground; and he was liable, therefore, to defeat by the mere swiftness, apprehension, and agility of a Lloyd George. There can seldom have been a statesman of the first rank more incompetent than the President in the agilities of the council chamber. A moment often arrives when substantial victory is yours if by some slight appearance of a concession you can save the face of the opposition or conciliate them by a restatement of your pro-

posal helpful to them and not injurious to anything essential to yourself. The President was not equipped with this simple and usual artfulness. His mind was too slow and unresourceful to be ready with *any* alternatives. The President was capable of digging his toes in and refusing to budge, as he did over Fiume. But he had no other mode of defense, and it needed as a rule but little maneuvering by his opponents to prevent matters from coming to such a head until it was too late. By pleasantness and an appearance of conciliation, the President would be maneuvered off his ground, would miss the moment for digging his toes in, and, before he knew where he had been got to, it was too late. Besides, it is impossible month after month in intimate and ostensibly friendly converse between close associates, to be digging the toes in all the time. Victory would only have been possible to one who had always a sufficiently lively apprehension of the position as a whole to reserve his fire and know for certain the rare exact moments for decisive action. And for that the President was far too slow-minded and bewildered.

He did not remedy these defects by seeking aid from the collective wisdom of his lieutenants. He had gathered round him for the economic chapters of the Treaty a very able group of business men; but they were inexperienced in public affairs, and knew (with one or two exceptions) as little of Europe as he did, and they were only called in irregularly as he might need them for a particular purpose. Thus the aloofness which had been found effective in Washington was maintained, and the abnormal reserve of his nature did not allow near him anyone who aspired to moral equality or the continuous exercise of influence. His   fellow-plenipotentiaries were dummies; and even the trusted Colonel House, with vastly more knowledge of men and of Europe than the President, from whose sensitiveness the President's dullness had gained so much, fell into the background as time went on. All this was encouraged by his colleagues on the Council of Four, who, by the break-up of the Council of Ten, completed the isolation which the President's own temperament had initiated. Thus day after day and week after week, he allowed himself to be closeted, unsupported, unadvised, and alone, with men much sharper than himself, in situations of supreme difficulty, where he needed for success every description of resource, fertility, and knowledge. He allowed himself to be drugged by their atmosphere, to discuss on the basis of their plans and of their data, and to be led along their paths.

These and various other causes combined to produce the following situation. The reader must remember that the processes which are here compressed into a few pages took place slowly, gradually, insidiously, over a period of about five months.

As the President had thought nothing out, the Council was generally working on the basis of a French or British draft. He had to take up, therefore, a persistent attitude of obstruction, criticism, and negation, if the draft was to become at all in line with his own ideas and purpose. If he was met on some points with apparent generosity (for there was always a safe margin of quite preposterous suggestions which no one took seriously), it was difficult for him not to yield on others. Compromise was inevitable, and never to compromise on the essential, very difficult. Besides, he was soon made to appear to be taking the German part and laid himself open to the suggestion (to which he was foolishly and unfortunately sensitive) of being "pro-German."

After a display of much principle and dignity in the early days of the Council of Ten, he discovered that there were certain very important points in the program of his French, British, or Italian colleague, as the case might be, of which he was incapable of securing the surrender by the methods of secret diplomacy. What then was he to do in the last resort? He could let the Conference drag on an endless length by the exercise of sheer obstinacy. He could break it up and return to America in a rage with nothing settled. Or he could attempt an appeal to the world over the heads of the Conference. These were wretched alternatives, against each of which a great deal could be said. They were also very risky—especially for a politician. The President's mistaken policy over the Congressional election had weakened his personal position in his own country, and it was by no means certain that the American public would support him in a position of intransigency. It would mean a campaign in which the issues would be clouded by every sort of personal and party consideration, and who could say if right would triumph in a struggle which would certainly not be decided on its merits? Besides, any open rupture with his colleagues would certainly bring upon his head the blind passions of "anti-German" resentment with which the public of all allied countries were still inspired. They would not listen to his arguments. They would not be cool enough to treat the issue as one of international morality or of the right governance of Europe. The cry would simply be that, for various sinister and selfish reasons, the President wished "to let the Hun off." The almost unanimous voice of the French and British press could be anticipated. Thus, if he threw down the gage publicly he might be defeated. And if he were defeated, would not the final peace be far worse than if he were to retain his prestige and endeavor to make it as good as the limiting conditions of European politics would allow him? But above all, if he were defeated, would he not lose the League of Nations? And was not this, after all, by far the most important issue for the future happiness of the world? The Treaty would be altered and softened by time. Much in it which now seemed so vital would become trifling, and much which was impracticable would for that very reason never happen. But the League, even in an imperfect form, was permanent; it was the first commencement of a new principle in the government of the world; truth and justice in international relations could not be established in a few months—they must be born in due course by the slow gestation of the League. Clemenceau had been clever enough to let it be seen that he would swallow the League at a price.

At the crisis of his fortunes the President was a lonely man. Caught up in the toils of the Old World, he stood in great need of sympathy, of moral support, of the enthusiasm of masses. But buried in the Conference, stifled in the hot and poisoned atmosphere of Paris, no echo reached him from the outer world, and no throb of passion, sympathy, or encouragement from his silent constituents in all countries. He felt that the blaze of popularity which had greeted his arrival in Europe was already dimmed; the Paris press jeered at him openly; his political opponents at home were taking advantage of his absence to create an atmosphere against him; Eng-

land was cold, critical, and unresponsive. He had so formed his *entourage* that he did not receive through private channels the current of faith and enthusiasm of which the public sources seemed dammed up. He needed, but lacked, the added strength of collective faith. The German terror still overhung us, and even the sympathetic public was very cautious; the enemy must not be encouraged, our friends must be supported, this was not the time for discord or agitations, the President must be trusted to do his best. And in this drought the flower of the President's faith withered and dried up.

Thus it came to pass that the President countermanded the *George Washington,* which, in a moment of well-founded rage, he had ordered to be in readiness to carry him from the treacherous halls of Paris back to the seat of his authority, where he could have felt himself again. But as soon, alas, as he had taken the road of compromise, the defects, already indicated, of his temperament and of his equipment, were fatally apparent. He could take the high line; he could practice obstinacy; he could write Notes from Sinai or Olympus; he could remain unapproachable in the White House or even in the Council of Ten and be safe. But if he once stepped down to the intimate equality of the Four, the game was evidently up.

Now it was that what I have called his theological or Presbyterian temperament became dangerous. Having decided that some concessions were unavoidable, he might have sought by firmness and address and the use of the financial power of the United States to secure as much as he could of the substance, even at some sacrifice of the letter. But the President was not capable of so clear an understanding with him-

self as this implied. He was too conscientious. Although compromises were
now necessary, he remained a man of
principle and the Fourteen Points a contract absolutely binding upon him. He
would do nothing that was not just and
right; he would do nothing that was
contrary to his great profession of faith.
Thus, without any abatement of the verbal inspiration of the Fourteen Points,
they became a document for gloss and
interpretation and for all the intellectual
apparatus of self-deception, by which, I
daresay, the President's forefathers had
persuaded themselves that the course
they thought it necessary to take was
consistent with every syllable of the
Pentateuch.

The President's attitude to his colleagues had now become: I want to
meet you so far as I can; I see your difficulties and I should like to be able to
agree to what you propose; but I can
do nothing that is not just and right, and
you must first of all show me that what
you want does really fall within the
words of the pronouncements which are
binding on me. Then began the weaving
of that web of sophistry and Jesuitical
exegesis that was finally to clothe with
insincerity the language and substance
of the whole Treaty. The word was issued to the witches of all Paris:

Fair is foul, and foul is fair,
Hover through the fog and filthy air.

The subtlest sophisters and most hypocritical draftsmen were set to work, and
produced many ingenious exercises
which might have deceived for more
than an hour a cleverer man than the
President.

Thus instead of saying that German-
Austria is prohibited from uniting with
Germany except by leave of France

(which would be inconsistent with the
principle of self-determination), the
Treaty, with delicate draftsmanship,
states that "Germany acknowledges and
will respect strictly the independence of
Austria, within the frontiers which may
be fixed in a Treaty between that State
and the Principal Allied and Associated
Powers; she agrees that this independence shall be inalienable, except with
the consent of the Council of the League
of Nations," which sounds, but is not,
quite different. And who knows but that
the President forgot that another part of
the Treaty provides that for this purpose
the Council of the League must be
unanimous.

Instead of giving Danzig to Poland,
the Treaty established Danzig as a
"Free" City, but includes this "Free"
City within the Polish customs frontier,
entrusts to Poland the control of the
river and railway system, and provides
that "the Polish Government shall undertake the conduct of the foreign relations of the Free City of Danzig as well
as the diplomatic protection of citizens
of that city when abroad."

In placing the river system of Germany under foreign control, the Treaty
speaks of declaring international those
"river systems which naturally provide
more than one State with access to the
sea, with or without transshipment from
one vessel to another."

Such instances could be multiplied.
The honest and intelligible purpose of
French policy, to limit the population of
Germany and weaken her economic system, is clothed, for the President's sake,
in the august language of freedom and
international equality.

But perhaps the most decisive moment, in the disintegration of the President's moral position and the clouding of
his mind, was when at last, to the dis-

may of his advisers, he allowed himself to be persuaded that the expenditure of the Allied Governments on pensions and separation allowances could be fairly regarded as "damage done to the civilian population of the Allied and Associated Powers by German aggression by land, by sea, and from the air," in a sense in which the other expenses of the war could not be so regarded. It was a long theological struggle in which, after the rejection of many different arguments, the President finally capitulated before a masterpiece of the sophist's art.

At last the work was finished; and the President's conscience was still intact. In spite of everything, I believe that his temperament allowed him to leave Paris a really sincere man; and it is probable that to this day he is genuinely convinced that the Treaty contains practically nothing inconsistent with his former professions.

But the work was too complete, and to this was due the last tragic episode of the drama. The reply of Brockdorff-Rantzau inevitably took the line that Germany had laid down her arms on the basis of certain assurances, and that the Treaty in many particulars was not consistent with these assurances. But this was exactly what the President could not admit; in the sweat of solitary contemplation and with prayers to God he had done *nothing* that was not just and right; for the President to admit that the German reply had force in it was to destroy his self-respect and to disrupt the inner equipoise of his soul; and every

instinct of his stubborn nature rose in self-protection. In the language of medical psychology, to suggest to the President that the Treaty was an abandonment of his professions was to touch on the raw a Freudian complex. It was a subject intolerable to discuss, and every subconscious instinct plotted to defeat its further exploration.

Thus it was that Clemenceau brought to success, what had seemed to be, a few months before, the extraordinary and impossible proposal that the Germans should not be heard. If only the President had not been so conscientious, if only he had not concealed from himself what he had been doing, even at the last moment he was in a position to have recovered lost ground and to have achieved some very considerable successes. But the President was set. His arms and legs had been spliced by the surgeons to a certain posture, and they must be broken again before they could be altered. To his horror, Mr. Lloyd George, desiring at the last moment all the moderation he dared, discovered that he could not in five days persuade the President of error in what it had taken five months to prove to him to be just and right. After all, it was harder to de-bamboozle this old Presbyterian than it had been to bamboozle him; for the former involved his belief in and respect for himself.

Thus in the last act the President stood for stubbornness and a refusal of conciliations. . . .

Harold Nicolson: PEACEMAKING, 1919

As the son of a British diplomat, Harold G. Nicolson was born in Persia and reared in various British embassies abroad. For twenty years he was himself in the foreign service of his country and attended the Peace Conference as a member of the English delegation. His writings have ranged from journalism to biography, history, and the novel. In Peacemaking, 1919, *Nicolson traced the course of his own disillusionment with Wilson's approach to international affairs.*

ON January 8, 1918, came the Fourteen Points.

Much casuistry, and some wit, has been expended upon these historic pronouncements. President Wilson himself referred to them in 1919 as "certain clearly defined principles which should set up a new order of right and justice." On the very same day we find Mr. Balfour writing of them as "certain admirable but very abstract principles." Yet were they so very abstract? Considering the date at which they were first issued, the Fourteen Points are precise to the point of recklessness. It may be well to summarise them as follows:

Speech of January 8, 1918.
"The programme of the world's peace, therefore, is our programme, and that programme, the only possible programme, as we see it, is this:

(1) "Open covenants of peace openly arrived at, after which there shall be no private understandings of any kind, but diplomacy shall proceed always frankly and in the public view."

(2) "Absolute freedom of navigation upon the seas outside territorial waters alike in peace and in war. . . ."

(3) "The removal, as far as possible, of all economic barriers. . . ."

(4) "Adequate guarantees given and taken that national armaments will be reduced to the lowest point consistent with domestic safety."

(5) "A free, open-minded and absolutely impartial adjustment of colonial claims based upon a strict observance of the principle that in determining all such questions of sovereignty the interests of the populations concerned must have equal weight with the equitable claims of the Government whose title is to be determined."

(6) "The evacuation of all Russian territory. . . ." "Russia to be given unhampered and unembarrassed opportunity for the independent determination of her own political development and national policy." Russia to be welcome, "and more than welcome" in the League of Nations "under institutions of her own choosing" and to be given every form of assistance.

(7) Belgium to be evacuated and restored.

(8) France to be evacuated, the invaded portions "restored" and Alsace-Lorraine returned to her.

(9) "A readjustment of the frontiers of Italy should be effected along clearly recognisable lines of nationality."

(10) "The peoples of Austria Hungary . . . to be accorded the freest opportu-

From Harold Nicolson, *Peacemaking, 1919*, pp. 38–44, 195–207. Reprinted by permission of the author.

nity for autonomous development."
(N.B.—This point was subsequently mod-
ified to provide for complete independence in lieu of autonomy.)

(11) Rumania, Serbia and Montenegro
to be evacuated, occupied territories to
be "restored." Serbia to be given free
access to the sea.

(12) Turkish portions of Ottoman Empire to be assured "a secure sovereignty."
Subject nationalities to be assured security and "absolutely unmolested opportunity of autonomous development."
Freedom of the Straits to be guaranteed.

(13) Independent Polish state to be
erected "which should include territories
inhabited by indisputably Polish populations, which should be assured a free and
secure access to the sea."

(14) A general association of nations
to be formed under specific covenants
"for the purpose of affording mutual
guarantees of political independence and
territorial integrity to great and small
States alike."

To the Fourteen Points themselves
must be added the "Four Principles" and
the "Five Particulars." The former were
contained in an address of February 11,
1918, and were prefaced by a statement
that the eventual peace should contain
"no annexations, no contributions, no
punitive damages." The Principles themselves can be summarised as follows:

(1) "Each part of the final settlement
must be based upon the essential justice
of that particular case."

(2) "Peoples and provinces must not
be bartered about from sovereignty to
sovereignty as if they were chattels or
pawns in a game."

(3) "Every territorial settlement must
be in the interests of the populations
concerned; and not as a part of any mere
adjustment or compromise of claims
among rival states."

(4) "All well-defined national elements shall be accorded the utmost satisfaction that can be accorded them without introducing new, or perpetuating
old, elements of discord and antagonism."

The "Five Particulars" figure in an address of September 27, 1918. They are
less illuminating. The first insisted on
justice to friends and enemy alike. The
second denounced all "separate interests." The third provided that there
should be no alliances within the body
of the League and the fourth forbade all
economic combinations between League
members. The fifth "Particular" reaf-
firmed the prohibition against secret
treaties.

Not only did I believe profoundly in
these principles, I took it for granted
that on them alone would the treaties
of peace be based. Apart from their inherent moral compulsion, apart from the
fact that they formed the sole agreed
basis of our negotiation, I knew that the
President possessed unlimited physical
power to enforce his views. We were all,
at that date, dependent upon America,
not only for the sinews of war, but for
the sinews of peace. Our food supplies,
our finances, were entirely subservient
to the dictates of Washington. The force
of compulsion possessed by Woodrow
Wilson in those early months of 1919
was overwhelming. It never occurred to
us that, if need arose, he would hesitate
to use it. "Never," writes Mr. Keynes,
"had a philosopher held such weapons
wherewith to bind the Princes of the
world."

He did not use these weapons. He was
not (and the slow realisation of this was
painful to us) a philosopher. He was
only a prophet.

*   *   *

Let me anticipate at this moment. Let me leave myself driving, wedged between despatch boxes and tin deed-boxes, from the Gare du Nord on that January 3, 1919, towards the Hotel Majestic. Let me contrast the principles enunciated by the Fourteen Points with the extent to which those principles were embodied in the eventual treaties of peace.

Our covenants of peace were not openly arrived at: seldom has such secrecy been maintained in any diplomatic gathering. The freedom of the seas was not secured. So far from free trade being established in Europe, a set of tariff-walls were erected, higher and more numerous than any known before. National armaments were not reduced. The German colonies were distributed among the victors in a manner which was neither free, nor open-minded, nor impartial. The wishes, to say nothing of the interests, of the populations were (as in the Saar, Shantung and Syria) flagrantly disregarded. Russia was not welcomed into the Society of Nations, nor was she accorded unhampered freedom to develop her own institutions. The frontiers of Italy were not adjusted along the lines of nationality. The Turkish portions of the Ottoman Empire were not assured a secure sovereignty. The territories of Poland include many people who are indisputably not Polish. The League of Nations has not, in practice, been able to assure political independence to great and small nations alike. Provinces and peoples were, in fact, treated as pawns and chattels in a game. The territorial settlements, in almost every case, were based on mere adjustments and compromises between the claims of rival states. Elements of discord and antagonism were in fact perpetuated. Even the old system of secret treaties was not entirely and universally destroyed.

Of President Wilson's twenty-three conditions, only four can, with any accuracy, be said to have been incorporated in the treaties of peace . . .

*   *   *

The collapse of President Wilson at the Paris Peace Conference is one of the major tragedies of modern history. To a very large extent that collapse can be attributed to the defects of his own intelligence and character. It is necessary to examine these defects and to relate them to the errors both of strategy and tactics which he committed.

"He possessed," writes Colonel House, "one of the most difficult and complex characters I have ever known." The bewilderment with which, in Paris, his blindness and irresolution filled those who were closest to him, is reflected in the extravagant explanations which they seek to devise. Mr. Stannard Baker, for instance, goes to all lengths to prove that Woodrow Wilson was the victim of a conspiracy on the part of the old diplomacy. Mr. Lansing, more equable in his judgment, implies that the apotheosis conferred upon the President after he landed in Europe upset the poise of his mind. Others have gone so far as to suggest that the constant twitching of the left side of his face, the illness which, under the guise of influenza attacked him in April, was an early symptom of that paralysis which was to strike him down in October. Be that as it may, the fact remains that the defects of President Wilson's character, his rigidity and spiritual arrogance, became pathologically enhanced after his arrival in Europe. They loomed as almost physical phenomena above the Conference of Paris.

It cannot be said that Woodrow Wilson underestimated the importance of his mission to Europe or the determinant role which he personally would be expected to play. He may, as Colonel House suggests, have looked forward to the Conference as to "an intellectual treat." Yet he was fully conscious of the immense responsibility devolving on him, fully aware of the appalling difficulties with which he would have to cope. He visualised himself (and in this, at that date, was no illusion) as the prophet of humanity, as an ambassador accredited to righteousness by all the world. "If," he proclaimed on landing, "we do not heed the mandates of mankind, we shall make ourselves the most conspicuous and deserved failures in the history of the world."

It would be inaccurate, in spite of such emotionalism, to regard Woodrow Wilson solely as a demagogic mystic who believed that a few sentences of English prose would at a breath demolish the ancient parapets of Europe. I have already emphasised his mystic, even his superstitious, side. His childish belief in the personal relation between himself and the number 13 is as trivial as his conception of the voice of the "plain people" as being identical with the judgment of God is an important manifestation of his mysticism. Yet he had his practical aspects. He warned the members of the delegation when addressing them in the saloon of the *George Washington* that the battle before them would not be easy. He warned them in the words of Josiah Quincy that they must fight for the new order, "agreeably if we can, disagreeably if we must." Mr. Lansing, it is true, condemns the President for his unbusinesslike methods, for his lack of programme or co-ordination. "From first to last," he writes, "there was no team work, no common counsel, and

no concerted action." Such a criticism, if I may venture the remark, might have applied to others among the plenipotentiaries. As compared with his colleagues at the Council table, Mr. Wilson was fully practical, admirably informed, perfectly precise. Mr. Balfour used frequently to assure us that there was no fault to be found with the President's technique. In conference he was invariably patient, conciliatory, calm. He was a trifle slow-minded at moments, but then he was dealing with the swift arrows of Clemenceau's Latin intellect, with the kingfisher dartings of Mr. Lloyd George's intuition. The collapse of Woodrow Wilson must be ascribed to causes far deeper than any lack of diplomatic technique or conference equipment.

The President, it must be remembered, was the descendant of Covenanters, the inheritor of a more immediate Presbyterian tradition. That spiritual arrogance which seems inseparable from the harder forms of religion had eaten deep into his soul. It had been confirmed in the course of many battles with the Faculty of Princeton. His vision had been narrowed by the intensive ethical nurture which he had received: he possessed, as he himself admitted, "a one-track mind." This intellectual disability rendered him blindly impervious, not merely to human character, but also shades of difference. He possessed no gift for differentiation, no capacity for adjustment to circumstances. It was his spiritual and mental rigidity which proved his undoing. It rendered him as incapable of withstanding criticism as of absorbing advice. It rendered him blind to all realities which did not accord with his preconceived theory, even to the realities of his own decisions. He and his conscience were on terms of such incessant intimacy that any little disagreement between them could easily be arranged. The profound, rigid, and quite justified conviction of his own spiritual rectitude; the active belief that God, Wilson and the People would triumph in the end; led him to look upon his own inconsistencies as mere transient details in the one great impulse towards right and justice. He identified the Covenant of the League of Nations with this his central impulse, and before the Ark of the Covenant he sacrificed his Fourteen Points one by one. Let it be hoped that the final clouding of his brain spared him the horror of understanding either what he had done to Europe, or what the American politicians had done to him.

His spiritual arrogance, the hard but narrow texture of his mind, is well illustrated by his apparent unawareness of political reality coupled with his distressing awareness of party reality. On the one hand he refused, for party reasons, to associate with himself any outstanding figure among his political opponents. Mr. Henry White, though a Republican, was not the representative which the Republican Party would themselves have chosen. The extreme bitterness with which Woodrow Wilson regarded all political opponents is one of the least agreeable, or prudent, traits in his character. On the other hand, although a violent party enthusiast, he seems to have been strangely blind to his own position in politics. He informed the members of his delegation in a solemn address delivered on board the "George Washington" that not only would America be the only disinterested nation at the Conference, but that he himself was the only plenipotentiary possessed of a full mandate from the people. "The men," he said, "whom we are about to deal with, do not represent their own people." Yet

at that very moment elections were in progress in England which were to send Lloyd George to Paris with a popular mandate more overwhelming than any recorded. M. Clemenceau, a few days later, obtained in the French Chamber a vote of confidence of four to one. Whereas Mr. Wilson himself, as the result of the elections of a month before, was faced with an actual majority against him in both houses of Congress. His refusal to confront these facts indicated a mind narrowing down to the exclusion of all outside light. It indicated (and there can be few better exhibits) that his mind was illumined only by the incense of his own self-worship; God-worship; people-worship.

As happens to most theocrats, Woodrow Wilson was a solitary and exclusive man. As is the case with many people possessed of active Presbyterian consciences, he was secretive, even towards himself. "He never," so records his most ardent supporter, "seemed to appreciate the value of mere human contact." "He appeared," says Mr. Lansing, "to consider opposition a personal affront." He was very willing to apply to his own admirable experts for information: he was seldom prepared to listen to them when they ventured to tender advice. In this predilection for the information of his experts in preference to their ideas, President Wilson was not unique among the plenipotentiaries of the Conference. Nor can we blame them; there were so many ideas: there was so much information: inevitably the plenipotentiaries, overwhelmed as they were, preferred to select from the latter those elements which accorded best with their own conception of the former. This common tendency among the plenipotentiaries accounts for the divergence of opinion expressed by the United States experts when cross-examined by their own Senate upon this very point. Mr. Lamont, one of the most unassailable figures at the Peace Conference, stated that the President consulted freely. Yet Mr. Lamont was a financial and economic expert and the President did not, in such matters, aspire to personal knowledge. Mr. Lansing, on the other hand, who was juridically and politically minded, contends that he took no counsel at all. "It was," he writes, "an entirely personal matter with him." In this, at least, President Wilson was on a par with his colleagues. The insistence of his critics upon his inability to consult his experts is not, I think, a very valuable insistence. . . .

*   *   *

"The world," thus had the President addressed his future coadjutors in the expectant smoking-room of the *George Washington*, "The world will be intolerable if only arrangements ensue; this is a Peace Conference in which arrangements cannot be made in the old style." Having delivered this pronouncement, Woodrow Wilson wallowed in arrangements as a tourist agent wallows in cross-country connections. Within a few days he had accepted an arrangement regarding the Brenner frontier. He allowed himself to be persuaded that war pensions could be classed as "damage to the civilian population." He allowed himself to believe that the mandatory system was in fact something different from annexation. He swallowed the war-guilt clause, and the grotesque clauses which arraigned perfectly innocent people among the war-criminals. He allowed the whole disarmament question to be "shunted off" into the realm of the onesided disarmament of Germany. He surrendered on Shantung, even as he surrendered on Poland. He surrendered

over the Rhineland, even as he surrendered on the Saar. On the reparation, financial and economic clauses he exercised no healthy influence at all, being, as he confessed, "not much interested in the economic subjects." He allowed the self-determination of Austria to be prohibited by one of the most specious phrases ever drafted by jurists. He permitted the frontiers of Germany, Austria and Hungary to be drawn in a manner which was a flagrant violation of his own doctrine. He said to his opponents, "I must stick by my principles, I ask you only to show me how your desires can be made to accord with my professions." And at the end of these tergiversations he continued to maintain that his original intentions had not, in fact, been infringed—that in the Covenant of the League could be found the whole cornucopia of blessings which he had undertaken to furnish to the world.

It never dawned upon him that in signing the Treaty of Guarantee with France he had dealt a blow to the prestige of his own Covenant from which that messianic doctrine was never to recover. Piteously he grasped at excuses for his own weakness. The Shantung settlement had been accepted to save the world from a new form of militarism. The Rhineland settlement had been agreed to in order to save the world from dislocation. "The great problem," he said on that occasion, "is the problem of agreement, because the most fatal thing that could happen, I should say, in the world would be that sharp lines of division should be drawn between the Allied and Associated Powers." "Personally," he added, "I think the thing will solve itself upon the admission of Germany to the League of Nations."

The Covenant, in fact, became for him the boxroom in which he stored all inconvenient articles of furniture. "There is," said Mr. Lansing, "in his mentality a strange mixture of positiveness and indecision. . . . Suddenness, rather than promptness, has always marked his decisions." These, surely, are manifestations of an essentially weak character. His transference of faith, away from the Fourteen Points and towards the Covenant, is another symptom of that inner insecurity. The League, however valuable it has been, and will be, as the clearing-house of international disagreements, could never have become, even had America adhered to it, a super-state directing all international activity. Mr. Wilson, having surrendered so much in the realm of fact, tried to recoup himself for these defeats in the realm of theory. Here again he was lacking in realism. "He gave them," writes Dr. Dillon, "credit for virtues which would have rendered the League unnecessary, and displayed indulgence for passions which made its speedy realisation hopeless." There must have been moments, towards the end of April, when President Wilson, despite his obscurantism, must have realised with anguish that he had made a muddle of his own doctrine. Yet with what torture of soul can he have reflected upon the increasing probability that the American people, that divinity in whom he trusted so blindly, would be the first to repudiate the only reputable work which he had accomplished?

It is frequently alleged that the least pardonable among President Wilson's errors was his failure to warn his associates that the United States might perhaps be unwilling to assume the obligation of supporting a system for the furtherance of which these same associates were being asked to make such heavy sacrifices of personal acquisition and security. Such an allegation is neither wholly accurate, nor wholly fair.

On the one hand the European powers were perfectly aware that President Wilson was not really representative of American opinion as it stood at the time. Early in January Mr. Lloyd George explained at a secret meeting of the British Empire Delegation the predicament in which he found himself. The Congressional elections of the previous November, the pronouncements of ex-President Roosevelt, the present attitude of the Senate, all indicated that America would not honour the blank cheque which Mr. Wilson desired Europe to accept in place of the older currency. Yet what was to be done? Constitutionally the President was still the spokesman and the chief executive officer of his country. Was it possible to inform him to his face that we distrusted his credentials? Obviously such a course was wholly impossible. The only thing which Europe could do was to save the face of the President; the only thing that Wilson would do was to save the face of Europe. Here, again, was a falsity of position which, although vital, has never been sufficiently stressed. Like most false positions it seemed too delicate for scientific or immediate probing. This particular abscess was never lanced.

On the other hand, President Wilson was not himself quite certain to what extent he would be repudiated by his own people. M. Clemenceau has recorded that when questioned regarding a possible change in American opinion the President "invariably replied with imperturbable confidence." "America," he said, "has taken much from me. She will take this also." "I admit," he informed the Supreme Council on March 20, "that the United States must assume the responsibilities, as well as take the bene-

fits, of the League of Nations. Nevertheless there is great antipathy in the
United States to the assumption of these
responsibilities." His optimism, as when
he contended in perfect seriousness that
the United States would accept a mandate for Armenia or even Constantinople, filled us with alarm. Yet it was not
wholly due to personal self-confidence.
It must be recollected that, in March of
1919, 34 of the 36 State legislatures and
33 governors had endorsed the League.
Even so hostile a critic as Mr. Lansing
admits that, so late as June 1919, "it was
a common belief that the President
would compose his differences with a
sufficient number of Republican Senators." It could not then be foreseen that
Mr. Lodge would be able to twist a
world responsibility into a partisan issue. The fact remains, none the less, that
after his visit to Washington in February, Mr. Wilson must have known that,
even if the Monroe Doctrine were in-
serted in the Covenant and thereby released America from all responsibility to
Europe, it was questionable whether the
Senate would ratify what he had done.
It might be contended, even, that it was
the realisation of this appalling fact

which induced him to surrender his principles to the desires of Europe. If this
be so, there is as yet no evidence to
prove it. Nor did the methods and manner of President Wilson before, and
after, his February visit differ from each
other to an extent which would justify
any such assumption. The fact, such as
it was, seemed too terrible to face. The
whole Treaty had been constructed on
the assumption that the United States
would be not merely a contracting but
an actively executant party. France had
been persuaded to abandon her claim to
a buffer state between herself and Germany in return for a guarantee of armed
support from the United States. The
whole reparation settlement was dependent for its execution on the presence on the Reparation Commission of
a representative of the main creditor of
Europe. The whole Treaty had been
deliberately, and ingeniously, framed
by Mr. Wilson himself to render American co-operation essential. Clearly, as
M. Capus had remarked in January, the
assumption and subsequent betrayal of
such responsibilities was a burden that
no human being could survive. Mr. Wilson did not survive it. . . .

Paul Birdsall:

VERSAILLES TWENTY YEARS AFTER—
A DEFENSE OF WILSON

For six years Paul Birdsall led an advanced seminar at Williams College in an investigation of "the diplomatic factors which shaped the general character of the Treaty of Versailles." In 1941 he published the results of these inquiries in a book which he believed "relevant to the immediate issues of war and peace, as they affect the United States and the world in general." Birdsall viewed the Peace Conference as a "struggle between Wilsonian principles of a new world order and the principles of reactionary nationalism." Obviously approving Wilson's program, he also made the most effective defense of Wilson's achievement in supporting that program at Paris.

IF the first World War taught us anything, it taught us that after four years of bloodshed democracies become thoroughly vindictive toward the enemy who has caused them to suffer. The peoples of England and France were in a mood to "hang the Kaiser" and to "squeeze the orange until the pips squeak." It is by now a commonplace that a hysterical populace in Allied countries called for punishment and destruction of Germany, and Allied leaders, true to the principles of democracy, bowed to the storm. Belief in the unique guilt of the Kaiser for the horrors of the World War was unanimous. Can the peoples of Great Britain and France entertain many doubts about the guilt of Hitler? If they could regard the people of Imperial Germany as "Huns" and barbarians, how will they think of their Nazi enemies?

How can such passions be controlled? They must be controlled if democracy is to solve the problem of a stable peace and of a durable world order. Only in a stable world can democracy survive. Those who decry idealism and justice as sentimental and unrealistic terms in world politics miss the point. For idealism and justice are the very rudiments of common sense. They amount to a practical realization of what the traffic will reasonably bear. They require the sacrifice of immediate vengeance for the sake of long-term enlightened self-interest.

Woodrow Wilson symbolized the forces of reason in the fight for a peace of justice. He spoke too much the language of idealism and self-sacrifice and too little the plain language of a genuine community of interest, and to that extent he brought upon himself the misrepresentation which obscured his real rôle in the Paris Peace Conference and contributed to the defeat of his program in the United States. A hardboiled and disillusioned age is quick to gibe about cant and hypocrisy, and Keynes' characterization of the Presbyterian theocrat who was "bamboozled" by Clemenceau and Lloyd George and could not be "de-bamboozled" has found recent echoes in Harold Nicolson's references to the "arid revivalism" of the "American Prophet," in whose pronouncements Nicolson observed "a slight tinge of revivalism, a touch of Methodist arrogance, more than a touch of Presbyterian vanity."

The simple thesis of such writers is that the doctrinaire and unrealistic program of Wilson collapsed under the impact of the power politics of Europe. Nationalist aims triumphed over his principles. There was division of the spoils of war, "bartering about of peoples and provinces from sovereignty to sovereignty as if they were chattels or pawns in a game," in defiance of his principle of self-determination. Worst of all, there had to be pretense. The Allied governments had accepted Wilson's program. While violating it, still they must pay it lip-service and hence, according to Keynes, they joined with Wilson in weaving "that web of sophistry and Jesuitical exegesis that was finally to clothe with insincerity the language and substance of the whole Treaty." Keynes in his disillusionment has fixed the legend of a Carthaginian peace in Wilsonian disguise.

This is caricature, not history, but like most successful caricature it has enough verisimilitude to be plausible. Scarcely as much can be said for Lloyd George's recent *Apologia*, which presents the exactly opposite thesis that Versailles was a purely Wilsonian peace. Only he does not call it Wilsonian, because it was he, Lloyd George himself, who achieved the peace of justice practically single-handed. Always adept at sleight of hand, in his latest masterpiece he demonstrates that he achieved Wilson's program in spite of Wilson. Like most commentators, he deplores the choice of war-worn

Paris as the seat of the Peace Conference, but hastily adds, "I cannot point out that in the sequel the purely Parisian influence made any serious impression on the actual stipulations of the document finally agreed to, since *I cannot discover a single particular in which it has departed from the terms of peace laid down by the Allies before the War came to an end.*" That statement acquires a peculiarly fine flavor of irony from the fact that Lloyd George himself bears major responsibility for the most egregious breach of faith contained in the entire treaty. The "Reparation" chapter of the Treaty of Versailles, besides being a clear violation of the Pre-Armistice Agreement with Germany, proved in the outcome to be the most disastrous section of the treaty. Keynes spoke with authority and even with clairvoyance on that subject.

The prosaic truth is that elements of good and bad were combined in the treaties. There were Carthaginian features like the Reparation settlement and Wilsonian features like the League of Nations. There was actually a distribution of colonial spoils of war, but only after the valuable principle had been established that colonial powers administered their new estates under specified conditions and subject to review and correction by an international tribunal, the League of Nations. The territorial settlement in Europe was by no means the wholesale, iniquitous, and cynical perversion of Wilson's principle of self-determination which has been pictured.

Harold Nicolson has explained many of the worst boundary decisions as resulting from sheer lack of coördination between the various expert commissions charged with a supremely difficult task. Yet most critics of the settlement forget the difficulties of that task. One of the commonest criticisms is directed against the shattering of the former Dual Monarchy of Austria-Hungary into those fragments called the Succession States. In this view the negotiators at Paris should have foreseen the economic and political need of a Danubian Confederation to combine the fragments. Yet Austria-Hungary had fallen apart before the Peace Conference convened and *de facto* national governments ruled the pieces. British and American delegates in Paris actually proposed a customs union for the area, only to encounter Italian objection, based on the principle of "divide and rule."

The populations of central Europe are hopelessly mixed, and therefore simon-pure self-determination is impossible. Any boundary will leave national minorities on one side or the other. Moreover, the history of the past few years has certainly justified the commissioners in taking account of strategic factors in the award of boundaries to the new states of Europe. The aftermath of the Munich settlement proved that Czechoslovakia could not exist without possession of its historic and strategic boundaries in the Bohemian mountains, even if that area is inhabited by 3,000,000 Germans. It is equally clear that a special status for the purely German city of Danzig, involving segregation from the political structure of the German Reich, is essential to the security of the Polish Corridor, which on the basis of pre-war German statistics is "indisputably" Polish territory. Hitler's demand for the reincorporation of Danzig in the German Reich was accompanied by a demand for territory across the Corridor itself. To have granted the demand for Danzig would have left the way open for the "fourth and final partition of Poland," even without the formality of war.

If the Allies should ever conquer Germany again, the negotiators of the new Versailles will face precisely the same dilemma. They can simply accept the traditional German thesis that Slavic peoples as an inferior racial breed have no right to independent national existence and permit Germany to rule Poland, Bohemia, Moravia, and Slovakia, or, if they acknowledge any right of self-determination to these peoples, they must inevitably violate in some degree the rights of German minorities. Hard as it is to visualize in 1941, it would not be surprising if the negotiators of the new Versailles were to recreate Poland and Czechoslovakia within something like the original Versailles boundaries.

In any case, it is well to be reminded by Professor Seton-Watson that it was not directly the Great Powers which profited from the partition of former German and Austro-Hungarian territory, but those new Slavic states which had themselves been partitioned and dominated for centuries. If their sense of injury was deep and their territorial appetite greedy in 1919, those sentiments are not likely to be extinguished by their present plight. If they received an unduly large measure of sympathy from the victorious Great Powers at that time, they would again secure at least their due share.

Finally, the territorial settlement contained in the various treaties negotiated at Paris is still, with all its faults, the closest approximation to an ethnographic map of Europe that has ever been achieved. If the next Peace Conference does better, it will be because of the achievements as well as the mistakes of Versailles. It can scarcely hope to do better unless some leading figure is prepared to undertake the rôle of Woodrow Wilson in restraining the forces of ex-

travagant nationalism. It will take a
brave man to assume that rôle.

AMERICAN PROPHET

President Wilson's own claims were
modest. When the rough and tumble of
negotiation was over in early June, 1919,
he said to the entire American delegation, "though we did not keep them [the
British and French] from putting irra-
tional things in the treaty, we got very
serious modifications out of them. If we
had written the treaty the way they
wanted it, the Germans would have gone
home the minute they read it. Well, the
Lord be with us."

Unfortunately, purely negative accomplishments, the prevention of positive
harm, rarely attract public attention. Yet
the record of what Wilson prevented is
just as important as his one great positive achievement, the League of Nations,
which, however dead at this moment, is
certain to be revived in some form in the
event of another Allied victory over Germany. The story of Wilson's struggle to
restrain nationalist demands is equally
important for an understanding of the
problems of the next Peace Conference.
Unless his successor is even better
equipped to cope with the forces of reaction, the second chapter of the League
of Nations can hardly have any happier
ending than the first. An understanding
of Wilson's difficulties will be the beginning of wisdom for anyone bold enough
to reënact his part.

The difficulties began before Wilson
sailed for Paris, reactionary nationalism
being equally at home on both sides of
the Atlantic. To Wilson it seemed particularly strong in the ranks of the Republican Party. Naturally, though unwisely, he invited the American electorate to return only faithful Democrats

to Congress, on the assumption that they
alone could be counted upon to support
his program. This purge, like a more recent one in American history, failed to
come off. Republicans captured control
of both branches of the legislature in the
elections of November, 1918, and the
most conspicuous and bitter opponent of
Wilson's program—Henry Cabot Lodge
—became chairman of the Senate Committee on Foreign Relations. Lodge's
lifelong friend, Theodore Roosevelt, interpreted the election for the benefit of
the nationalists of Europe:

Our allies and our enemies and Mr. Wilson himself should all understand that Mr.
Wilson has no authority whatever to speak
for the American people at this time. His
leadership has just been emphatically repudiated by them. The newly elected Congress comes far nearer than Mr. Wilson to
having a right to speak the purposes of the
American people at this moment. Mr. Wilson and his Fourteen Points and his Four
Supplementary Points and his Five Comple-
mentary Points and all his utterances every
which way, have ceased to have any shadow
of right to be accepted as expressive of the
will of the American people. . . .

Acceptance of the Wilsonian principles referred to had become a contract
between the Allied and Associated Powers on the one hand and Germany on the
other, as a condition for the granting of
an armistice and the convening of a
Peace Conference. In effect, Roosevelt
was inviting the Allied governments to
repudiate their pledges to both President Wilson and the German Government. Though noisy, Theodore Roosevelt was only a private citizen. It was
one thing for him to announce that the
American people had themselves rejected the whole contractual basis for

peace. It was quite another for his friend Henry Cabot Lodge, as Chairman of the Senate Committee on Foreign Affairs, to indulge in similar pronouncements. On December 21, 1918, less than a week after Wilson's arrival in Paris, the *Congressional Record* published the substance of Lodge's speech to the Senate, in which he advised Europe that what it did to Germany was no concern of the United States. Let the Allies administer a severe peace to leave Germany disabled and helpless, and exact heavy indemnities. No attention need be paid to Wilson's principles with regard to new boundaries in Europe, for that was none of his business. Above all, postpone all plans for the construction of a League of Nations until Germany had been summarily disposed of.

The alliance of reactionary nationalisms in Europe and America undermined Wilson's position from the start. The alliance was tacit but real. Colonel House records that "the elections of last November have been a deterrent to free action by our delegates," and Lloyd George is smugness itself in describing the contrast between his own and Wilson's position. Lloyd George enjoyed an overwhelming popular mandate, and knowing the weakness of Wilson's position, could be nonchalant about Wilson's threats to appeal to public opinion. "His occasional threats to appeal to American opinion, when he did not get his way at the Conference, conveyed no real menace. There was no assurance that his country would support him in a break with the Allies on any issue."

Many writers have commented on this initial handicap, but few have bothered to analyze the more subtle and complicated difficulties created by the behavior of the American delegation at the Peace Conference. It is notorious that Secretary of State Lansing was hostile to the whole idea of a League of Nations as contrary to American traditions of isolation, and that he logically joined forces, at a later date, with the Republican "Irreconcilables" to wreck the peace settlement. Wilson, at least, knew where Lansing stood and therefore excluded him from any appreciable part in the peace negotiations. The rôle of Colonel House, the President's closest friend and most intimate adviser, is so difficult to estimate that it is still clouded by controversy. This much, at least, is clear. He was so devoted to one part of the President's program—the establishment of a League of Nations—that he was willing to sacrifice almost any amount of the rest of that program to reach his goal. He was so afraid that Italy, or Japan, or France, or even Great Britain, would refuse to join the League of Nations, that he was ready to satisfy their nationalist ambitions for territory or indemnities in order to be assured of their support. He would "satisfy the greedy ones by giving them what they want." House was, moreover, a genial man with a flair for human relations, and much too adroit for either his own or Wilson's good. He got on with Europe's leaders far better than the President, and they formed the habit of using him as their intermediary when Wilson proved stiff and difficult. They constantly explained to him that, unlike the President, he was a diplomat to his finger-tips, and the Colonel's diary for this period shows that he was not wholly immune to this form of flattery. Indeed, one of his colleagues among the American Commissioners, the professional diplomat Henry White, goes so far as to suggest that House became the unwitting ally of European nationalism.

White's letter to Lansing of November 8, 1919, deserves fairly full quotation:

I was not aware until recently of the extent to which intrigue went on "upstairs" during the earlier months of the Conference, with a view to preventing any of the views of our experts, which happened to be contrary to those held there, from reaching the President. Still less had I any idea of the attempts made to get some of the experts to change their views and adopt those advocated in the small upper chamber previously mentioned.

Since your departure I have realized more and more how grievously misled the Italians and others were by the tendency to compromise and by the assurances of friendship and sympathy, of a general nature at least, if not actually with their particular views, expressed during their interviews upstairs: and there is no doubt in my mind that Fiume and other questions would have been settled while the President was still here, if they had been left in your hands or kept in the President's, and had not been hampered by a feeling upstairs that no decision should be attempted, much less reached, which would in any way be likely to cause jeopardy to the adoption of the League of Nations Covenant . . .

Under these circumstances and in view of the undue influence which I cannot but think our British friends exercise over our late colleague, I cannot help feeling anxious . . . about participation in the League of Nations if we are to be represented there by a man . . . given to compromise and not strong enough and willing to make a fight in which our interests (which besides being commercial are those of world peace as against special national interests such as land-grabbing and sphere-of-influence capturing, now rife in Europe) are likely to be overridden unless carefully guarded and defended. . . .

It is only fair to add that, in part, the Colonel's behavior is to be explained by a deep and entirely natural sympathy with the sufferings of France and the other victims of German arms. It was a sympathy widely shared by the American experts of the Peace Delegation, and however chivalrous its basis, it greatly complicated Wilson's task by making him seem ungenerous. Clemenceau openly accused the President of being pro-German on one issue where even Wilson's own experts were against him. One of the most usual complaints against Wilson made by European writers is this same lack of sympathetic understanding, in contrast to the greater warmth of other members of the American delegation. In case after case he held out against concessions urged upon him by the experts and Colonel House.

What, then, is the true picture of the man who tried against such odds to maintain his principles? Undermined at home, imperfectly supported by his own colleagues in Paris, his frequent refusals to compromise may well have seemed the inflexible rigidity of an arid revivalist or the arrogance of a prophet. The harsh lines of the caricature fade out in the kindlier and more realistic portraiture of Henry White, and White's portrayal is all the more convincing because of the absence of any natural bonds of affinity between himself and Wilson. A professional diplomat with thirty years' experience of old-world diplomacy, he was scarcely an eager disciple of any prophet of a new world order. Republican Party affiliations and a lifelong friendship with Senator Lodge ought to have kept him immune from too much sympathy for Wilson. Yet this is what he wrote his friend, Representative Rogers, from Paris on April 7, 1919:

I have discovered since knowing him that he is really shy, and in an atmosphere which he does not feel to be entirely sympathetic, much more in one which is antagonistic, his reserve increases in proportion to the absence of sympathy. That he has a very human side there is no doubt, and I have also found him at various times attractive . . . I have also noticed that he is much more "get-at-able" in conversation with one other person: whether on account of his natural shyness or what, I do not know . . . certainly when we talk to him as a Delegation, he is apt to do most of the talking, whereas when I see him alone, I have found him a very good listener and apparently appreciative of what is said to him. I suppose it is for that reason that he deals so much with and through Colonel House, rather than taking advantage of the collective information of all those by whom he is immediately surrounded; whether it be the Peace Conference or his own Cabinet at home.

When one considers the deplorable lack of understanding available in Paris, the President's reputation for stiffness is more readily understood. It was not the stiffness of prophet or revivalist, but the protective covering for the sensitiveness of an academic temperament. Lloyd George is, therefore, much nearer the mark when he abandons talk of the missionary and the theocrat, and contrasts the toughness of his own hide with Wilson's sensitiveness, because the President's nerves had not been "hardened for the stinging and scorching arrows that burn and fester in the ruthless conflicts of a political career." It is clear why Lloyd George did not regard Wilson as "comparable to his great rival, Theodore Roosevelt."

For all the weaknesses of the academic temperament, Wilson remained a man of courage in the face of almost insuperable obstacles. White admitted that he became more and more impressed with the greatness of that quality, and he re-

peatedly sought to impress upon Senator Lodge that "dignity and distinction" characterized everything which Wilson did in Europe. He tried in vain to convince Lodge of the soundness of the President's program and begged him not to wreck it. He maintained that Wilson's activity in Europe had vastly increased American prestige.

WHAT PRICE A LEAGUE OF NATIONS?

The cardinal point of Wilson's program was its most vulnerable spot. The Allied premiers well knew Wilson's determination to establish a League of Nations in the treaties themselves as the cornerstone of a new world system, and they were not scrupulous in exploiting that determination to extract concessions from him. Henry White suggests that Colonel House was responsible personally for fatal concessions to nationalist greed in order to purchase support for the League, but he has said more generally of Wilson:

The fact is that the League of Nations in which he has been more deeply interested than anything else from the beginning . . . has been played to the limit by the French and Japanese in extracting concessions from him; to a certain extent by the British too, and the Treaty as it stands is the result. The Italians overshot the mark.

That remark is the most valuable clue to the labyrinthine maze of Peace Conference negotiations that has yet been offered. It may be true, as Harold Nicolson has said, that there was no recognizable pattern of negotiation, that in the confusion and fog of Paris there was "amazing inconsequence, the complete absence of any consecutive method of negotiation or even of imposition." Yet it is extraordinary what a clear scheme of diplomatic strategy emerges from the fog, once the major territorial and other problems are studied in relation to the contemporaneous negotiations in the League of Nations Commission.

It was one thing to secure acceptance of the principle that there should be a League of Nations in the treaty. It was quite another to expect the states of Europe to adopt any particular constitution of a League that Wilson might formulate. Indeed, he was wise enough to avoid the presentation of any cut-and-dried proposition of his own. The actual construction of a League was bound to raise fundamental questions affecting the sovereign rights of all nations, and the Great Powers, at least, had the right to decide as to what provisions should or should not be embodied in the charter to which they were invited to subscribe. The negotiations which dealt with the actual text of the Covenant in the League of Nations Commission were a magnificent opportunity for obstruction. French, Japanese, or even British representatives in the Commission could press their own proposals, or withhold assent to Wilson's, not necessarily on the merits of the proposals themselves, but for the sake of "nuisance value" or bargaining advantage.

Wilson's dilemma was serious enough without such complications. He must devise a Covenant which would genuinely assure America's support to a system of collective security, without at the same time too patently violating American traditions of isolation. A small group of Senate "Irreconcilables" led by Senator Lodge was determined to reject any League of Nations which Wilson could devise, and he must at all costs avoid giving them the ammunition with which to compass that destruction. He must, therefore, resist French and Japanese proposals which would seem to endow

the League with the authority of a superstate to restrain the exercise of sovereign rights by member states. He must equally secure the adoption of American provisions explicitly safeguarding certain distinctively American rights, like the Monroe Doctrine, as sacred and inviolable.

On both fronts the President was in a peculiarly vulnerable position. Too much restraint on the authority of the League, either from resistance to French and Japanese proposals or from insistence on American reservations, would justify the foreigner in saying that such a League afforded him no security and that he must, therefore, look to more tangible guarantees. Since these tangible guarantees usually involved an annexationist scheme totally at variance with the rest of Wilson's program, the horns of his dilemma were particularly sharp. This dilemma is the clue to the maze of Peace Conference diplomacy. . . .

Design for Diplomacy

First, chronologically and logically, came the claims of certain of the British Dominions—supported by the British delegation—to annex former German colonies in Africa and in the Pacific. Such claims were a direct challenge to Wilson's proposal that all the former German colonies become the property of the League of Nations, to be administered by mandatory powers chosen by the League and subject to its supervision. There was as yet no League and there was certainly no code for Wilson's mandatory principle that could be regarded as binding the Dominions. Their acceptance of the mandatory principle was necessarily contingent upon some concession to their demand for direct and unconditional control of former German territory. They were willing to sell their support to a League of Nations Covenant including the mandate principle—at a price.

Next, logically, appeared the Japanese program. It included annexationist aims in the Pacific, which had to be accorded the same consideration which the Dominions' claims received. More serious were the extensive ambitions of Japan on the mainland of China. Her claims to rights formerly exercised by Germany in the Shantung province raised grave problems about the place of China in a new world order. They constituted a direct challenge to Wilson's program. Yet, at the same time, Japan presented a perfectly reasonable request for explicit recognition of the equality of races in the League of Nations Covenant. While reasonable enough in the abstract, this proposal was defeated by the practical consideration that it might possibly endow the League of Nations with authority to dictate to member states about their immigration legislation in cases where it discriminated against particular races. Could Japan be expected to submit to defeat on both the racial question and Shantung? No account of the Shantung settlement is complete without attention to the concurrent negotiations of the Japanese delegates in the League of Nations Commission.

Most important of all was the French program, since it was the most extensive, the most clearly articulated, and by far the most dangerous challenge to Wilson's program. The French program envisaged the permanent disruption and subjugation of the German Reich. It comprised a variety of individual items which, taken together, form a remarkably consistent pattern, and the separate items gained additional coherence from the directing genius of Clemenceau who personally coordinated the negotiations

of the French delegates by a single strategic plan. The essence of that plan was to press for amendments to the League of Nations Covenant which Wilson was bound to oppose, and to oppose American amendments which Wilson was bound to press—ostensibly for the sake of French security, actually to create bargaining power. The chapter which deals with the policy of Bourgeois and Larnaude in the League of Nations Commission is not only essential to an understanding of the deep divergence between Anglo-American and French mentality; it also forms a necessary introduction to the study of individual aspects of the French program. Succeeding chapters deal with French proposals for the disarmament of Germany; for the endowment of Poland with maximum territories at the expense of Germany in the east; for the creation of a buffer state out of Germany's Rhineland provinces in the west; for the annexation of the Saar Valley; for the exaction of the entire cost of the war from Germany.

In every phase of these negotiations—with the British concerning colonies and mandates, with the Japanese concerning Shantung, above all with the French in every particular of their national demands—Colonel House was active and conciliatory. His concern for the League, sharpened by his experience in the League of Nations Commission, his anxiety about protracted negotiation in a chaotic world, his intimacy with the Allied premiers, especially Clemenceau, led him to adopt an "appeasement" philosophy. On every major issue he advocated compromise and concession at the expense of the accepted principles of peace, and in every case beyond definite limits set by Wilson. To this extent he assisted the strategy of the British, Japanese, and French in extracting concessions from Wilson, although in every instance except that of the Reparation Settlement Wilson successfully stopped short of the extremes of compromise to which the Colonel was urging him. Yet in both substance and method Colonel House's negotiations with the Italian delegation proved a climax of appeasement philosophy. They revealed a rift within the American delegation, cutting deep to roots of philosophy and method; they led to an open break with the Italian delegation; and they apparently ended the Colonel's own relations of mutual trust and confidence with President Wilson. Fiume and its consequences are symbolic of the deeper reasons for the failure of a new world order to emerge from Versailles. The Fiume episode, though distinct from the Versailles negotiations, forms an appropriate conclusion for any analysis of the diplomatic factors which shaped the general character of the treaties at the end of the first World War. . . .

WHO WERE THE REALISTS?

The intellectual nihilism of the twenty years since Versailles has destroyed faith in the Wilsonian program at Paris. By misrepresenting the character of the treaty, the motives that inspired it, above all by denial of any genuine American stake in European settlement, it has provided the strongest moral force by which Hitler "softens" his victims before striking them down with physical force. The disillusioned liberal has been the unwitting ally of the cynical advocate of physical force as the only conceivable basis for world politics.

In such an atmosphere, any constructive effort like Wilson's is bound to appear silly and unrealistic. The romantic liberal must see the immediate realization of his hopes or turn on the author of his hopes with charges of betrayal, and those who have thoroughly cynical reasons for opposing a new order will welcome the charges. The statesman who labors for the best constructive results obtainable in a chaotic world starts under the terrible handicap of a war on two fronts: against cynical opposition, and equally against his sentimental and perfectionist supporters. At Paris the situation was complicated by the fact that the American delegation contained not merely representatives of the simon-pure liberal school, but advocates of the opposition itself, not in any cynical sense, but because they were so profoundly impressed with political realities as they existed that instinctively they thought in terms of compromise beyond the limits of any real necessity.

In this welter of conflicting viewpoints it has recently become fashionable to eschew all standards of judgment and to resort to the methods of social psychology in describing the melee. The result has the pleasingly remote, detached, and scientific atmosphere of a study in anthropology. It becomes a study in abstraction and determinism, and involves no issues or principles with which any reader need concern himself. It is both the realistic and the scientific method applied to the writing of history, and it reinforces the intellectual nihilism of the disillusioned liberal.

Is it really scientific in taking account of all the data within the particular field of its concern? The only thing this method leaves out is the set of standards and principles which men themselves accepted as the basis upon which they agreed to work, and thereby accepted as the standards by which they might legitimately be judged. The only element which gives coherence and significance to the study of the Paris Peace Conference is the set of principles with reference to which it acted, the degree to which it embodied them in the treaties, the extent to which it departed from them, and the reasons—personal and political—for the result. No account which ignores or prejudges that frame of reference can claim to be scientific.

To assume at the outset that the Fourteen Points were unreal and impractical, incapable of being translated into concrete terms of peace, ignores the simple fact that they constituted a legal contract between the Allied and Associated Powers and Germany to govern the terms of peace. It is just as unrealistic to impugn the intelligence and integrity of the Peace Commissioners who took the contract seriously in the first place as to denounce them all indiscriminately as hypocrites who systematically violated principles in which they never believed, or as fools who could not recognize the violation of a principle when they committed it. The contract was there as the basis of all their efforts. It was a reasonably ascertainable contract, the details of application admittedly difficult, but by no means so impossible as many writers have alleged. It is quite possible to distinguish between the degrees of good faith and intelligence brought to the task by the different national delegations at Paris, as it is possible to distinguish the degrees of intelligence and good faith within the personnel of any one of these delegations. Such treatment must, obviously, take account of the real political pressures upon men by national tradition and public opinion. To ignore the necessity of reasonable compromise in political affairs is just as fatal to realism as to assume that, all politics being of the essence of compromise, there are no rules at all and no standards of judgment but those of immediate political success.

It is an extraordinary fact that as yet there has been no balanced interpretation of Peace Conference diplomacy to take the measure of all the factors involved. When a penetrating critic like Harold Nicolson undertakes to recall the discussion to a firm basis of reality by emphasizing the fundamental conflict of principle, he does so only to go off the deep end of romantic-liberal disillusionment, and produces a spiritual autobiography of his loss of faith in Wilson. In his reaction against the prophets and dreamers of the world, he embraces the realists who at least know the rules of the balance of power in Europe—for example, Eyre Crowe of the British Foreign Office and Colonel House, "the best diplomatic brain America has yet produced."

The issue of realism at Paris is mainly the question of the short-term as against the long-range view. The pressures of national demands, made effective and menacing through diplomatic strategy in the League of Nations Commission, made immediate and pressing by the danger of delay in pacifying a turbulent and disintegrating Europe, necessitated a degree of compromise. The realists of the American delegation lost their perspective under such pressure and were ready to throw away all their cargo in the scramble for the lifeboats. The cargo consisted of the Fourteen Points, the substance of the Pre-Armistice Agreement, the contract with Germany. Colonel House felt that if the boat were lightened sufficiently, it would still carry the League of Nations, but Harold Nicolson's description of a general *sauve qui peut* attitude in the later phases of the Peace Conference applies well to elements within the American delegation. In this atmosphere, one concession was an argument for the next.

Mezes could not see why the American delegation should "stand up so much straighter" on the Fiume question against the Italians than on other questions involving other powers; Colonel House advocated extreme concession to the Japanese on the ground that, although clearly a violation of principle, it was no worse than many other concessions which had already been made. There was little attempt to discriminate between detail and principle, between the relative merits of national demands, between the varying degrees of diplomatic strength which supported the demands. Above all, there was no thought save for the immediate future—make peace quickly and start the League of Nations. The realism of these men consisted in an abdication of sheer nerve and intelligence.

Naturally, President Wilson looked stiff and unrealistic when viewed through the eyes of such men, at the very time when William Bullitt was resigning from the American delegation in protest at Wilson's sacrifice of principle, and others were grumbling that the treaty was thoroughly bad. To the former group he seemed rigid and uncompromising, to the latter weak and uncertain in his stand on principle. A careful study of the record reveals an extraordinary consistency in Wilson's fight for his program under overwhelming difficulties, as well as a high degree of political intelligence in translating the abstract principle of his program into concrete details of application.

The President's understanding of the real issues involved in the Saar case was superior to that of his own experts, and that was the only issue where he stood completely alone against everyone in Paris. In the Polish case, he was convinced by the arguments of Lloyd George as to the long-term results of a settlement based on the Polish Commission's report and loyally supported Lloyd George's efforts to modify that settlement in the face of the Polish sympathies of the American experts. He withstood steadfastly Colonel House's pressure to compromise on the colonial question, the Rhineland, the Saar, the Adriatic. His worst defeats were the Reparation settlement and Shantung; the first occurred while Wilson was ill, when Colonel House abandoned the American program; the second, because of an impregnable political and diplomatic position held by the Japanese.

Throughout the conference Wilson maintained his stand on principle as the only safe guide in a welter of conflicting interests, as the sole safeguard against laying foundations for future conflict. That was the meaning of his attempt to force an admission from Colonel House that the pro-French proposals of the American experts for the Saar Valley were a violation of the Fourteen Points. The record for the crucial April period is eloquent testimony to the President's perspective and force, and Fiume is the final symbol. In the nature of the case, Wilson's role—aside from the arduous work in the League of Nations Commission—had to be negative rather than constructive, to concern itself with prevention rather than cure. Consequently the failure of his curative and constructive work, as the result primarily of American refusal to ratify the treaty and enter the League of Nations, has obscured the real nature of his achievement at Paris. It is so much easier to record failures than to carry through the laborious task of assessing a man's work by careful measurement of what he prevented, as well as by study of positive achievements.

Perhaps the most general criticism President Wilson has encountered, at the time and since, has been on the score of his decision to attend the Peace Conference in person. The decision itself was attributed to excessive vanity, and the effect has generally been described as the degradation of the remote and lofty, almost godlike arbiter to a bloody and battered contestant in the European prize ring. The assumption is that Wilson in Washington could have retained his detachment with an ultimate power of decision while delegating the rough-and-tumble of negotiation to Colonel House in Paris. It is interesting that Secretary Lansing and Colonel House, who agreed upon practically nothing else, should have consistently concurred on the unwisdom of the President's coming to Paris. Independently, they tried in advance to prevent it; subsequently, they communed over the misfortune of the event. Yet, in view of Lansing's attitude toward Colonel House, it is difficult to imagine his acquiescing in the Colonel's primacy in Paris. It is possible that each man in the assurance of his own superior wisdom felt confident of exercising greater influence in Wilson's absence.

The present book affords the most positive answer on this point. The record clearly shows that on every major question but that of Reparation, the Treaty of Versailles would have been a worse treaty had Wilson remained in Washington. With all his mistakes, he emerges as the only man of real stature at Paris.

His fight for ratification—when he returned to the United States—is another story and another Wilson. The strain of his intensive speaking campaign on behalf of ratification superadded to the long strain of the struggle in Paris, brought a physical collapse. After the stroke of paralysis, in October 1919, he became readier prey to the tactics of the Senate Irreconcilables, whose game was so to amend and denature the League Covenant that the author himself would reject his own handiwork. At the very moment when French and British officials indicated their willingness to accept the denaturing amendments for the sake of continued American collaboration in Europe, Wilson gave the fateful order of rejection:

I shall consent to nothing. The Senate must take its own medicine. . . .

Thomas A. Bailey:

WOODROW WILSON AND THE LOST PEACE

*Thomas A. Bailey, Professor of American History at Stanford, af-
firms: "I happen to be among those who believe that history has lessons for those who will read." For this reason he has recently turned
his scholarship and his lively style to studies of the role of public opinion in shaping foreign policy and to the history of American-Russian
relations. A similar motive prompted him in 1944 to an extensive examination of Wilson's conduct at Versailles. In approaching this subject Bailey noted: "I must at the outset confess to a great admiration
for many of Wilson's qualities, and to complete sympathy for the broad
ends that he sought to attain." These sentiments did not, however,
keep Bailey from stressing what he thought were "the most costly blunders made by the negotiators."*

A GREAT many people still think of
the Covenant of the League of Nations and the Treaty of Versailles as two
separate instruments. This, of course, is
incorrect. The League of Nations Covenant was incorporated in the Treaty of
Versailles as Section I. Not only was it
placed at the very first, but considerable
portions of the rest of the pact were so
interwoven with it that the United
States Senate could not cut out the
Covenant without unraveling the whole
fabric.

This is of vast importance, for it is
clear that the League of Nations, with
its vulnerable Article X, was what defeated the Treaty of Versailles in the
United States. To put it another way, if
the Covenant had been a separate instrument the Treaty would almost certainly have been approved by the Senate.

We have already seen that Wilson
won two great diplomatic victories during his first month in Paris. The first was
wringing from the Conference an acceptance of the mandate principle. The
second was forcing the detailed Covenant of the League of Nations into the
text of the Treaty. This represented a triumph over those who wanted to postpone consideration of the League to
the indefinite future, notably the French,
and those who wanted merely to outline
the general principles of a League in the
Treaty. This latter view initially commanded much support from the British.

Wilson regarded the League as the
"key to the whole settlement," and from
the start he favored the bodily incorpo-
ration of the Covenant in the Treaty. He
encountered some opposition, chiefly
from the French, but in the end he was
able to have his way. It was a great personal triumph for him when, on January
22, 1919, the Council of Ten went on
record as favoring his plan, and three
days later the plenary session formally
and unanimously gave its approval to

the integral idea in the very first resolution of the Conference.

This unanimity does not mean that there was tremendous enthusiasm for the League. Wilson had made it clear, notably in his Manchester reply to Clemenceau's balance-of-power speech, that acceptance of the League was the price that Europe would have to pay for America's cooperation in the peace settlement. The price seemed small indeed for the benefits that the wealthy United States could confer on a sick and impoverished Europe. One usually humors a rich uncle.

The efforts of Wilson to secure an acceptance of the League as an integral part of the Treaty have erroneously been pictured as a last-ditch struggle against the wicked powers of the Old Order. While it is clear that Clemenceau had little desire to put the League first, it is true that Wilson received considerable support from the British, who actually drafted the resolution adopted by the Council of Ten and strongly supported it in the plenary session. But it is significant that the original resolution read that the League should be a "part of the peace." Wilson objected. This might mean that his pet project would in some vague manner be associated at a later time with the entire peace settlement, and this in turn might mean that the League would be sidetracked. He promptly proposed an amendment to read that the League should be "an *integral* part of the general treaty of peace." The amendment carried without difficulty.

One need not overdramatize Wilson's part in this episode to conclude that he must bear the major part of the responsibility for forcing the Covenant bodily into the Treaty of Versailles.

We must note at the outset that there were powerful arguments for Wilson's position. The League was the Fourteenth Point—the capstone point—and he could conceive of neither a satisfactory treaty nor a lasting peace without the Covenant's being the heart of the whole arrangement. He believed that liberal opinion throughout the world, which had rallied to his stirring war aims, would be profoundly disappointed if he should bring home from Paris the corpse of a treaty which did not include the League—a League that would smooth out the inevitable imperfections of the entire pact.

Not only would the League be the keystone of the edifice but, if adopted in principle at the outset, it would strike the keynote of the Conference—a clarion call for the new order. It would also facilitate the making of the rest of the Treaty, for—to take only one example—if a puissant League existed to maintain order, there would be less need of haggling over such problems as strategic frontiers.

A great many of the European leaders, especially those of lesser rank, rather mildly favored the League of Nations; but they generally regarded it as of secondary importance when compared with the urgent necessity of making peace with Germany. Once this was done, and the spoils were divided, and the enemy was enchained, it would be in order to draw up a League in a leisurely fashion —a powerful League which would make sure that the Allies could keep what they had taken away from their fallen foe. The problem was merely one of first things first. "Why," it was currently asked, "should the roof be put on before the foundations are solidly laid?"

This argument was unanswerable—if Wilson could take it for granted that when the loot was parceled out, and the

Treaty signed, the weary delegates would not pigeonhole the League and go home. Yet this was precisely what he could not take for granted. He knew that neither Lloyd George nor Clemenceau really believed in the League. Clemenceau not only had sneered at it quite openly, but had, as we have noted, come out unabashedly for the old balance of power. The French delegation at the Conference had the League last on their agenda.

It is true that the security-obsessed French would have been enthusiastic about the League if they could have had the kind of arrangements they wanted: a League of Allies rather than a League of Nations. From first to last they fought for an international army under League jurisdiction, preferably with a French general in command, or at least an international general staff, which could take vigorous action against Germany at the slightest sign of assertiveness. In other words, a powerful military machine for freezing the status quo, and keeping the heel of the victor permanently on the neck of the vanquished.

From first to last, Wilson fought this proposal. There were various objections to it, but one need only point to the fact that the Constitution of the United States puts the war-declaring power in the hands of Congress, not in those of an international body in Geneva. Wilson was amply warned by his advisers—and this must have been evident to him without such advice—that a treaty providing for an international police force would not have a ghost of a chance in the Senate. To paraphrase William Allen White, a superstate with a superarmy and a superstaff might even be tempted to knock the superdaylights out of the United States.

In short, the French conceived of the League as an instrument for perpetuating the military alliance of the victors, and they were quite willing to call it a League of Nations or a Society of Nations or any other name that would please Wilson. When Clemenceau found that the League might be forged into such an instrument, he ceased to sneer at it. But when it turned out to be a milk-and-water League, he had no enthusiasm for it. He felt that it was not totally useless, because it might add something to French defenses when taken in connection with other guarantees; but he placed no reliance on it, and would not accept it as a substitute for real security. One Gallic wit reflected a common view when he said that the League was "impossible" but "indispensable."

It is clear from all this that Wilson had unassailable grounds for believing that if the Covenant was not forced into the Treaty, it might easily be sidetracked for all time.

On the whole it seems as though Wilson's instincts and strategy were sound, though, as will become evident, the same cannot be said for his tactics. Like a great gambler, he was staking everything on a new world order and a new era of perpetual peace. If such a new world order were to be established, there would have to be a League; and the only way to be sure of a League, Wilson felt, was to have it in the Treaty.

Public opinion throughout the world seemed ripe for such an innovation. The time to strike was when the iron was hot. When the iron cooled off, and public opinion began to lose sight of the horrors of war and became absorbed in domestic reconstruction, enthusiasm for the League would undoubtedly wane, if not evaporate. The world in 1919 was hot and malleable; the time to reshape it was before it grew cold and hard.

We do not know what would have happened—we can only guess—if Wilson had been willing to postpone the League to a subsequent pact. We do know that he waged a determined fight to force it into the Treaty of Versailles, and that the whole Treaty was defeated by a narrow margin in the United States, largely if not primarily because it contained the League. But so many other factors contributed to this narrow defeat—a number of them much more foreseeable than this particular one— that it is hardly just to censure Wilson for it. One must repeat: Wilson was gambling for enormous stakes; the odds seemed to be not altogether unfavorable. If he won, he might win enormous benefits; if he lost, the world could hardly be worse off than it had been under the bankrupt old system of power politics.

But it does not seem to have entered Wilson's head at this stage of the game— and perhaps never—that he could lose. He simply took it for granted that the Senate would approve what he brought home, and he ill-advisedly assured his British and French colleagues at the Conference that this was so. He was confident that the American people would rise up in righteous wrath and not permit their representatives to defeat his Treaty. He did not believe that the Senate would dare incur the odium of committing so dastardly a crime against humanity. . . .

The decision to force the Covenant into the Treaty led to a train of tragic consequences. It necessitated a hasty and imperfect drafting; it introduced an element of distraction and confusion which diverted energy from the primary business of making peace with Germany. It tarred the Covenant with the black brush of Versailles, and caused neutrals to feel uncomfortable about going into a League which was embedded in a punitive treaty of peace. And finally, as already noted, the Covenant brought about the complete defeat of the Treaty in the United States, and in this way contributed powerfully to the collapse of the whole postwar settlement. All this, it seems, might have been avoided if Wilson had not stubbornly refused to accept a compromise between his point of view and that of his critics.

Certain leaders at Paris, including Secretary Lansing, Lord Robert Cecil, Colonel House, Arthur J. Balfour, and others, believed that the ideal solution was neither to postpone consideration of the League until after the Conference, nor to insert the Covenant bodily into the Treaty. Rather, there should be a general statement in the Treaty committing the signatories to the broad principles of a League, and making specific provision for the formation of a commission to erect the machinery in a saner and less hurried atmosphere.

Once the Senate had approved the Treaty, with the general outlines of the Covenant in it, and had sanctioned the creation of a commission to draw up the final instrument, the resulting League Covenant possibly could have been adopted by a simple executive agreement. In this case the Senate would have been by-passed, and Senators Lodge and Borah and Brandegee would not have had a chance to attach a long list of qualifying reservations.

In other words, the negotiators at Paris might have planted an acorn in the Treaty, with the expectation that it would grow into a lusty young oak in the sunshine of experience. As it was, they planted an oak and finally got only a sickly acorn.

The acorn-planting method undoubtedly had much to commend it. It would have prevented that sidetracking of the League which Wilson very properly feared. It would have avoided any serious delay, because the drafting of a few general principles would have taken little time and would have commanded general assent. It would have enabled neutral representatives to take part in the subsequent discussions. It would have given time for passions to cool, and would have made possible the deliberate working out of the specific problems in a more wholesome atmosphere.

Above all, a general statement of principles in the Treaty would have choked off hostile criticism in America. It would have given ample opportunity to the opponents and proponents of such a plan to advance their ideas—as co-authors if you will—for the guidance of those who were later to be charged with the task of drafting the League Covenant.

This is vastly important. General principles, as a rule, do not offer much for critics to attack. Everyone—or almost everyone—favors peace and good will toward men, and some measure of international collaboration toward that end. But when anyone advances specific and detailed plans for achieving those ends, the critic has something definite to sink his teeth into. He will raise questions and doubts; and questions and doubts tend to multiply in the minds of the public. Details were what ruined the League in America.

This does not mean that the Covenant was an unnecessarily wordy instrument. It was an admirably succinct and simple statement, in the tradition of the United States Constitution. Wilson was opposed to elaborate machinery, and insisted that it was the spirit of the thing that counted. Yet, even so, the Covenant was too detailed for its enemies. Some found it too strong, some too weak; some too vague, some too specific. A determined and jaundiced critic could find lurking in it all the hobgoblins he was looking for.

Why Wilson did not listen to Lansing and the others when they advanced the acorn-planting idea, one cannot say. He was a stubborn man, and did not compromise readily. He had made up his mind that the Covenant—a detailed Covenant—should go into the Treaty. And it did. . . .

*   *   *

What manner of treaty was Wilson carrying home for the hostile scrutiny of the United States Senate?

It has been fashionable in recent years to condemn the Treaty of Versailles as thoroughly bad. The truth is that it contained much that was good and much that was bad. We need not try to determine whether the good outweighed the bad; but, all things considered, it is remarkable that the defects were not more numerous, more pervasive, and more glaring. One could even go so far as to say that the most surprising thing about the Treaty is not that it was unsatisfactory but that any kind of treaty came out of the madhouse at Paris. Certainly no other conference was ever confronted with such a complex of problems, and certainly none has ever dealt with a comparable task more scientifically and expeditiously. As compared with other great conferences of the past, this one moved at a dizzy pace.

We have considered the blunders—at least some of the blunders—that the statesmen made. But in all fairness it must be pointed out that there were certain conditions over which the negotiators had no control whatsoever, and these conditions would have left their imprint on any peace at that time.

The vision of the delegates and of their people was clouded by the passions of a war that was still too close. The Peace of Versailles was almost literally negotiated on the ruins of a smoking battlefield. As Lloyd George told the House of Commons: "I am doubtful whether any body of men with a difficult task have worked under greater difficulties—stones crackling on the roof and crashing through the windows, and sometimes wild men screaming through the keyholes." The tragedy is that in order to win the war the Allies had been forced to whip up such passions at home as to make difficult if not impossible the winning of the peace. "Once lead this people into war," Wilson had said in 1917, "and they'll forget there ever was such a thing as tolerance."

The Bolshevik menace, rising like an ominous flood, cried aloud for haste. Its red rivulet licked into Hungary, into Bavaria. There was every temptation to build hastily and quickly, rather than permanently and well. "Better a bad treaty today," was the saying, "than a good treaty four months hence."

The situation in Central Europe was nothing short of chaotic. Succession states were rising like phoenixes from the ruins of the ramshackle Austro-Hungarian empire. They could not wait for the quiet dictates of the Conference; they moved in and took what they wanted, thus presenting the negotiators with accomplished facts. In many cases the oppressed became the oppressors, and all the more savage because of their soul-searing experience.

Men cried, "Peace! Peace!" but there was no peace. While the peacemakers were busy in Paris, the warmakers were busy in Russia and Central Europe. It would in fact be difficult to name a single year following the Armistice when a serious armed disturbance was not agitating some part of the world. Bonar Law told the House of Commons, a few days before the Germans signed the treaty, that twenty-three different wars were raging in various parts of the world. It was as if some giant monster, threshing about in death agony, had broken into twenty-three convulsive parts. No wonder men spoke cynically of "the terrors of peace."

Peace is not in itself a condition: it reflects a condition. We should never forget that one of the insuperable obstacles at Paris was that the frock-coated negotiators were expected to produce a settlement in lands where there was no settlement, in lands where their authority did not extend.

There were several other conditions over which the negotiators could have no control.

Behind everything and permeating everything were politics. Clemenceau, Lloyd George, and Orlando—yes, even Wilson—were but the servants and mouthpieces of their people. If they yielded too much, if they did not bring back the spoils of victory, they would be thrown out and replaced by men of sterner stuff. Clemenceau and Lloyd George generally tried to give the public what it wanted. They survived. Orlando failed to give the people what they wanted. He was unhorsed. Wilson tried to give the people what *he* wanted. He was broken.

Where there were so many clashing interests, there had to be compromise or there would be no settlement. The representatives of great nations will not voluntarily consent to sit down at a table and be outvoted by an unfriendly majority. Compromise between two groups is often difficult and always unsatisfactory; but at Paris there had to be compromise among four or five of the great powers, and this increased the difficulty and dissatisfaction vastly more than four- or five-fold. It was simply impossible for Wilson to have his own way all—or perhaps most—of the time, even though he had powerful economic weapons in his arsenal. The marvel is that he got as much of his program written into the Treaty as he did. The explanation probably is that the European nations, despite the muttering in the American press and the sniping in the Senate, did not realize the extent to which he was losing his hold on public opinion. Not a single one of the great powers was satisfied with the Treaty. This was because it had to be a compromise, and no compromise, as we have observed, is ever completely satisfactory to all the parties concerned. Each power felt that it had yielded too much and received too little. In France, Clemenceau was condemned as the dupe of Wilson and Lloyd George; in England, Lloyd George as the dupe of Wilson and Clemenceau; in America, Wilson as the dupe of Clemenceau and Lloyd George.

Another unavoidable difficulty at Paris was that the peace was a coalition peace, just as the war had been a coalition war; and a coalition can seldom move with complete singleness of purpose.

Napoleon once remarked that his brilliant victories had been easy because he was fighting a coalition of enemies. The Allies of 1914–1918 had prosecuted the war in a disorganized fashion, until the spring of 1918, and they framed the peace in a disorganized fashion, under the additional handicap of having disposed of the enemy who had forced them to unite. When we consider that it is on the whole a more delicate and complicated task to make an enduring peace than to prosecute a successful war, it is all the more surprising that the results were not less satisfactory.

Finally—and ominously—Russia, the blind Cyclops of the East, had no part in the Conference.

It is not altogether clear that this was an avoidable blunder. Russia was in the throes of one of the bloodiest civil wars in history, and it was impossible to tell which group of officials represented the nation. Wilson and others backed an attempt to bring the discordant elements together on the isle of Prinkipo in the Sea of Marmora; but this failed, partly because of Russian recalcitrance, and partly because of French opposition. It is probably true that the problem was an insoluble one, but the fact is that France ruined whatever scant prospects there were for success. She would have no traffic, in the colorful phrase of Winston Churchill, with the "foul baboonery of Bolshevism."

Repeated reference has been made in these pages to the Big Four. It was really the Big Five. Lenin was the fifth member—an invisible member occupying an invisible chair. He was more important than Orlando. He held the Conference to its labors, and applied the whip and spur. Russia was more important at Paris than Prussia; Prussia had no voice, Russia had a loud though ghostlike voice.

Thus the peace settlements of 1919 embraced only Western and Central Europe and Turkey, with due attention to Germany's overseas empire. The powers could delineate Poland's western borders; but they could not delineate her eastern borders. These could be settled only between her and Russia.

It seems self-evident that there can be no European settlement without Russia, for Russia is about one-half of Europe. It seems self-evident that there can be no world settlement without Russia, for Russia is about one-seventh of the world.

So it came about that peace—an uneasy peace—was made with only one side of Europe. The other side was still in chaos. The wonder is that the settlements lasted as long as they did.

Wilson at Paris conceived of the problem before him as a dual one. He tried to make peace with Germany, which was the immediate task, and at the same time reorder international relations, which was the long-run task. The two became hopelessly entangled, and neither was satisfactorily handled.

One of the results—and a fatal result —was that the Treaty of Versailles fell between two stools. It was neither a thoroughgoing victor's peace nor a peace of accommodation.

There are two ways of dealing with a fallen foe. The one is to make a peace so generous that he may forgive and forget. Whether Germany would have responded favorably to such treatment is still a matter of speculation, but there was a possibility that it might have worked. The second method is to impose a victor's peace, with the purpose of keeping the conqueror's heel on the enemy's neck as long as physically possible. This method is certain to breed another war.

The Treaty of Versailles contained some of the most severe terms that one civilized nation has ever imposed on another, while elsewhere it soared heavenward in the lofty idealism of the Covenant of the League of Nations. It was harsh enough to humiliate and anger

the Germans but not drastic enough permanently to enchain them—assuming that this could ever be done. It was idealistic enough to create the illusion of workable peace machinery, but selfish enough to make that machinery unworkable in a real crisis.

The seeds of war were planted by the statesmen at Paris in many of the articles of the Treaty, but in that impassioned atmosphere they knew not what they were doing. Before 1914, France was the aggrieved power, nursing memories of Alsace-Lorraine and vanished *gloire*, while preparing for a war of revenge; after 1919, Germany was the aggrieved power, nursing memories of Danzig and lost colonies and frustrated plans of European domination, while preparing for a war of revenge. The "guilt clause" was a verbal Alsace-Lorraine.

Wilson recognized that there were inequities in the Treaty, but he confidently counted on the League to iron them out at a later date and in a saner atmosphere. This was a splendid ideal, but utterly unworkable, because Article V of the Covenant called for a unanimous vote in the Assembly and Council on all questions of substance. France, Poland, and others could always be counted on to veto any proposition that would show leniency toward Germany or her vanquished satellites. This was one of the prices that Wilson had to pay for France's adherence to the League of Nations.

Wilson also had to yield to French insistence that Germany be kept out of the League, which she was until 1926. The opposition of France was natural, but it had the most unfortunate result of causing the League to appear like a new Anglo-French alliance—a kind of exclusive international club from which Germany was excluded because of her moral blemish. This weakened the League in the eyes of both Germany and the other non-member nations, and subjected it to an incessant barrage of criticism and denunciation.

In the final analysis the League of Nations turned out to be an organization designed to freeze the status quo and keep the victorious Allies permanently in the saddle. The League was in essence an alliance of the victors, without the binding force of a true alliance. It evolved into an organization designed not to create a new balance of power but to preserve the existing imbalance of power.

This, of course, was not what Wilson wanted. "You cannot go forward," he said, "with one foot in the Old Order and the other in the New." But this was the best he could bring back from Paris, and he hoped that it would work out better than it did. Ironically, the very concessions that he was forced to make in order to give life to the League were the very concessions that ultimately gave it death.

The New Order, far from being established, merely "fouled the Old"—to use the phrase of Harold Nicolson. In the view of many Europeans the idealistic bungler from America should have stayed at home and allowed the Europeans to make a good old-fashioned victor's peace. War probably would have followed, but perhaps it would have been delayed for two generations instead of one. Possibly that is the best humanity can hope for. But Wilson was unable to resign himself to such defeatism.

A strong point should be made of the fact that a large part of Wilson's achievement at Paris was purely negative. It can even be argued that his most important contribution was not what he did but what he prevented others from doing,

notably in connection with the Saar, saddling Germany with the entire cost of the war, and dividing Germany's colonies on a purely imperialistic basis, illusory though all of these solutions may have been.

It is true that many things went through which he did not approve. But there were so many iniquitous heads popping up at Paris that he could not tilt a lance at every one he saw. He concentrated his efforts on what he regarded—in some cases mistakenly—as the most iniquitous. It is worth repeating that the punitive parts of the Treaty undoubtedly would have been more harsh had he not been at Paris.

The critics of Wilson almost unanimously charge that his most conspicuous failure at Paris had to do with self-determination. Instead of Poles being forced to live under German domination, Germans were forced to live under Slavs, Slavs were forced to live under Italians. New if smaller minorities were seemingly exchanged for old.

Most conspicuous of all, the nearly seven million Germans of Austria were forbidden to join hands with their compatriots in Germany. The French, with their decimated man power and declining birth rate, found it unthinkable that Germany should emerge from this bloody war with a larger population of Germans than in 1914. Austria was to be made so independent that she could not exercise the right voluntarily to yield her independence. She was left an economic shell: a tremendous capital without a hinterland; a heart without a body. In all this Wilson reluctantly acquiesced.

The most glaring violations of the principle of nationality were in some instances avoidable, in others unavoidable. But on the whole the Paris settlement was a victory for self-determination.

This principle was far more often honored in the observance than in the breach. Many more millions of minority groups were released from alien domination than were consigned to alien domination. The result was the closest approximation that modern Europe has ever had to an ethnographic map coinciding with a political map.

This raises the question whether an ethnographic map was what Europe needed: whether it would not have been better to have fewer states rather than more, whether it would not have been better to have more economic self-sufficiency and less self-determination, less abstract justice and more economic viability. Man does not live by bread alone, but he cannot live without bread.

The critics of Wilson say that at Paris he sacrificed his Fourteen Points one by one in order to save the League, just as a mother would throw her younger children to the pursuing wolves in order to save her first-born. Harold Nicolson, at least by indirection, accuses Wilson of having abandoned nineteen of his twenty-three points and principles.

This statement is pure nonsense, but it should be examined to determine how intelligent men can arrive at so erroneous a conclusion.

Critics like Nicolson assume that because a point, like self-determination, was not fully achieved, it was completely betrayed: 90 per cent success is total failure. This, in all honesty, is unfair. Winston Churchill estimated that fewer than 3 per cent of the people of Europe were condemned to live under governments whose nationality they repudiated. On the whole, the territorial readjustments in Europe were the most reasonable part of the settlement, and they generally benefited the small states rather than the great powers.

Nicolson takes it for granted that because a point was not achieved at Paris, it was completely betrayed. This also is unfair. Wilson assumed, for example, that the League of Nations would take care of freedom of the seas, and he had confidence that the machinery specially set up by the League would deal satisfactorily with disarmament. It did not do so, but that was not because he betrayed his principles, but because others betrayed the League.

Certain other points could not be carried out at Paris, notably those having to do with Russia and Turkey, because the confusion in those places had not sufficiently subsided.

When we rule out Russia and Turkey, and consider what the League was supposed to do, and include those points that were in large part carried out either in letter or in spirit, we have a far different picture. This is why men like Secretary Lansing could honestly testify, after the Treaty of Versailles was signed, that in so far as circumstances then permitted, the Fourteen Points were "substantially" carried out. This could not have been said a few years later, but by that time a situation had developed over which Wilson could have no control.

Even so, the fact cannot be blinked that when the Germans laid down their arms they were tendered a solemn contract promising, with specified exceptions, the Fourteen Points. The contract did not say that the points would be "substantially" carried out, or carried out in so far as circumstances would permit. The contract was terribly binding; and from the German point of view no excuses were valid.

In any case, the word "betrayal" is far too strong when applied to Wilson and his Fourteen Points. There are errors of commission and errors of omission. Most of the criticism of Wilson is directed not at what he did but at what he failed to do. Most of his critics assume that he should have forced his Points fully and completely upon colleagues who did not want them, and who under no circumstances would accept them. Not even Wilson could do the impossible. The original error was to permit his name to be used in giving currency to the belief that he could.

Wilson was never willing to confess— and probably never believed—that he had betrayed his Points. He told the newspapermen before leaving Paris that he had secured more than he had expected when the Conference began, and he insisted that the general spirit of the Fourteen Points had permeated the discussions. As for betraying Germany, he declared to the very end that the Treaty was severe but just.

Allied apologists not only agreed with him on this last point, they also made much of the fact that the Treaty of Versailles was not so bad as that of Brest-Litovsk, which the Germans had imposed upon a vanquished Russia early in 1918.

This is all beside the point. It is true that Brest-Litovsk was a bad peace, so bad in fact as to provide unanswerable justification for the charge that the Germans would have dictated a Carthaginian treaty had they been the victors. But two wrongs still do not make a right. The task before the negotiators at Paris was not to pay off old scores, or to make a treaty as bad as Brest-Litovsk, or as bad as the Germans might have made had they won, but to construct a workable and lasting peace which both the victors and the rest of the world so desperately needed.

The Treaty of Versailles in general and Wilson in particular have been savagely blamed for many sins that they did not commit.

Much of the Treaty was concerned with righting century-old wrongs. A wrong that old sometimes ceases to look like a wrong. The aggressions of Prussia, for example, had netted her territory, notably in Poland, which on the basis of self-determination had to be taken away. Yet the eggs had long been scrambled, and the unscrambling process created newer but perhaps lesser wrongs. It was no easy problem to thrust back into Central Europe a populous nation which had passed out of existence during the Presidency of George Washington in America. The ghosts of those who had partitioned Poland in the eighteenth century stalked through the halls of Versailles.

The men of Paris were blamed for creating the quarrelsome "succession states" of Czechoslovakia, Jugoslavia, and Poland, all of which were destined to sow dragon's teeth of trouble in Central Europe. But the Conference did not create these states. They sprang into being before the negotiators could meet. The task at Paris was to delineate their boundaries and erect safeguards to insure that they would live in peace with their minorities and their neighbors.

The Treaty of Versailles has been blamed for all the ills that befell Europe from 1919 to 1939. The truth is that there had been a grueling, demoralizing conflict of more than four years' duration before the Conference met. It has been competently estimated that the war alone cost Germany $100,000,000,000. If the negotiators at Paris had been angels from heaven they could not have drawn up a treaty which would have prevented many of the calamities of exhaustion and reconstruction. Europe was sick, desperately sick; and Harold Nicolson is correct when he says that those who write about Versailles are not describing a conference but a serious illness.

Lloyd George insists that most of the sins of the Treaty must be laid at the doors of the men who carried it out—or who failed to carry it out. With all due allowance for exaggeration, we must concede that the former prime minister has put his finger on a fundamental truth. Commissions were to be set up, plebiscites were to be held, reparations were to be determined and collected. The Treaty in itself was no magic formula; no man-made document can be. Everything depended on the energy, intelligence, loyalty, broad-mindedness, and singleness of purpose of those who were charged with administering it. In many respects the executors of the Treaty are unquestionably far more censurable than its makers.

There is one final observation. The Treaty of Versailles—the treaty with Germany—was but one part of the European settlement. The treaties with Austria, Hungary, Bulgaria, and Turkey were intimately connected with it, just as Wilson had planned and later boasted. The very first section of every one of these treaties was the Covenant of the League of Nations. Not only was the Covenant the first section of the Treaty of Versailles, but other provisions of the same treaty were interlocked with it, and all the treaties were interlocked with one another. The Reparations Commission established by Versailles, for example, was charged with supervising the collection of reparations under the treaty with Austria.

The essential point is that the interlocking postwar settlements were a complicated and topheavy structure which could only endure if its most important foundation stone was put into place. The whole edifice was erected on the assumption, and with Wilson's assurances, that the United States would bear its share of the responsibility for guaranteeing the new world order. The Europeans did not like the architecture of the new building, but they accepted it as a cheap price for the cooperation of a powerful America.

The most important foundation stone, as we all know, was never put into place. The precarious structure teetered along for more than a decade, and then crashed in ruins.

If the Europeans had been told at the outset that they could not count on our support, they would have built a different structure. Whether it would have been better, one cannot say; but it would have been different, and perhaps it would have lasted longer.

We have already considered the blunders of the Paris negotiation at such length that their applicability to a future conference should be self-evident. But for purposes of re-emphasis and summary, it seems desirable to stress certain basic principles which the American people should keep in mind in connection with a general peace at the end of a great world conflict.

War aims should be unambiguous, practicable, acceptable to American public opinion, and closely correlated with the pronouncements of our allies.

The people should be so led during the conflict that their emotionalism will be held in leash. The greater the passions aroused by the fighting, the greater the difficulties in making a lasting settlement. One may win the war but lose the peace, as we did last time. The objective should be to pace one's self so as to win both.

American public opinion should be educated *in advance* to its responsibilities in world affairs, and more particularly to its responsibilities in executing the peace treaty. This campaign should be undertaken as early in the war as possible, for when the fighting ends the time is always too short for adequate instruction. Wilson made a heroic attempt to educate the country *after* the treaty was completed, but by that time the Senate had gained too big a head start.

Unconditional surrender on the part of the enemy is imperative, unless the conditions are defined with unmistakable clarity, unless they are capable of fulfillment, and unless the victors intend in good faith to fulfill them. Even so, unconditional surrender is no sure guarantee of an enduring peace.

The American peace commission should be bipartisan, with adequate representation accorded the two great political parties, as well as the Senate of the United States.

The President should enter into the closest and most cordial possible relations with the leaders of both parties in the Senate—*before, during* and *after* the negotiations.

A preliminary peace should precede the final treaty, and it should speedily outline the military and other terms most pressingly in need of solution. This will enable the world to adjust itself to a peacetime footing, while giving passions time to cool off. At a later date the negotiators can approach the general settlement with greater deliberation and clearer vision.

The defeated powers should be privileged to discuss, both orally and in writing, the terms of the definitive treaty *while they are being drawn up*. This is the only practicable way in which the reasons for the unworkability of certain provisions may be adequately set forth.

The detailed covenant for a new world organization, if any, should not be written into the treaty of peace. General provision may be made in the pact for creating some such system at a subsequent time and under different auspices. Making peace with the enemy should not be confused with making a constitution for a new order.

No treaty can last unless it provides *workable* machinery for peaceful change in the light of changing conditions.

The victor can have vengeance, or he may have peace, but he cannot have both. In 1919 the Allies got neither, for vengeance was incomplete and short-lived. No great nation can be kept in bondage forever. The vengeance of 1919 enlisted neutral sympathy, created a "remorse complex" in the minds of liberals in the victor nations, and revived German nationalism. Germany needed to be persuaded that war was bad; instead she was convinced that the peace was bad. All these factors contributed to the final undoing of the Treaty of Versailles.

The Constitution should be amended so as to reduce the great obstructive power of the one-third minority in the Senate. Opponents of any treaty are armed with two votes; the proponents with only one. This is illogical, undemocratic, and in 1919 it was probably disastrous. The same thing could easily happen again. The sooner the Constitution is changed the better because amendment takes time, and procrastination is easy. When treaty-making is not in prospect, the two-thirds rule seems unimportant; when it is in prospect, time is too short for amendment. If we wait for Congress to take steps to reduce its own power, we shall doubtless have to wait a long time. But the Constitution provides adequate machinery for the states to initiate and ratify amendments without the voluntary action of Congress.

The President of the United States should never again make promises which the Senate cannot reasonably be counted on to honor or public opinion to support. It will be a long time before the world recovers from the disillusionment of 1919.

The temple of peace must be built on the foundation of what people are likely to accept and what they will accept, not on what they should ideally accept.

Wilson had a noble vision but he made the tragic mistake of thinking that mankind, without the proper preparation and education, could attain a kind of international millennium at a single bound. As he told his associates on the *George Washington,* "If it won't work, it must be made to work." He assumed that human nature—with its suspicion, fear, selfishness, and greed—could be substantially changed overnight, especially American human nature. He took it for granted that our people would respond gladly to his gospel of unselfishness, speedily assume responsibilities commensurate with their new power, and willingly shoulder burdens from which they could expect no direct gains. Unto America much had been given; she should repay her debt to the rest of the world. It was to be a new era of joy through service.

Instead, we got Harding and "normalcy."

Statesmen must ever remember that mankind is shortsighted and perverse, and that he who would make haste too fast will almost inevitably fail. We shall not see the millennium in our day, or in our children's day; the best we can hope for is a substantial step forward on the tortuous path of international understanding and cooperation. If we can but learn the lessons from our last experience which are there for all to see, the price paid for them, though far too high, will not have been spent altogether in vain.

Richard Hofstadter: WOODROW WILSON: THE CONSERVATIVE AS LIBERAL

Richard Hofstadter, one of the most stimulating and perceptive writers among the rising generation of American historians, is a professor at Columbia University. His study of The American Political Tradition and the Men Who Made It *has been hailed for its fresh and critical examination of the major political figures in our history. The following critique of Wilson's peace program springs from Hofstadter's conviction, expressed in his Introduction, that "In a corporate and consolidated society demanding international responsibility, cohesion, centralization, and planning, the traditional ground is shifting under our feet." He believes, "A democratic society, in any case, can more safely be overcritical than overindulgent in its attitude toward public leadership."*

WILSON'S uncertain course during the neutrality period revealed two inconsistent strategic ideas. The first was that the United States must remain the Great Neutral, the conservator of sane and just peacetime values, the exponent of "peace without victory." The second was that the Allies must not be allowed to lose the war, that the "military masters of Germany" must be crushed.

This same contradiction pursued him to the Peace Conference. What he really wanted was not simply a "peace without victory," but a victory to be followed by an unvictorious peace. He wanted the Allies and Germany to come to the conference table as victors and vanquished and sit down as negotiators. Events soon impressed upon him the impossibility of any such thing. He told one of the American experts who accompanied him to Paris that "we would be the only disinterested people at the Peace Conference, and that the men whom we were about to deal with did not represent their own people." The second statement was in some ways an unhappy delusion, but the first was true: the United States, thanks in part to Wilson's restraining influence, was the only nation among the victors that came without a set of strictly national aims, without a single claim for territory, indemnities, or spoils, with the sole demand that the Allies restrain themselves in the interest of a just and more durable peace. The Conference was an affair of three sides—the victors, the vanquished, and Wilson.

In the absence of American claims, which might have been used for trading purposes, Wilson had two cards to play: the threat of a separate peace with Germany, and the financial supremacy of the United States. The mere hint of a separate peace by Colonel House in November 1918 threw the Allied representatives into consternation and precipitated their acceptance of the Fourteen

Reprinted from Richard Hofstadter, *The American Political Tradition and the Men Who Made It*, pp. 272–275. By permission of Alfred A. Knopf, Inc. Copyright 1948 by Alfred A. Knopf, Inc.

Points as the basis of the Armistice; but this threat was pushed no further. Wilson, just as he had failed to use his country's economic position to bargain with England over blockade practices, failed to use this advantage at the Peace Conference. Although he wrote to House, July 21, 1917:

England and France have not the same views with regard to peace that we have by any means. When the war is over we can force them to our way of thinking, because by that time they will, among other things, be financially in our hands,

this strategy also was neglected. A very large proportion of American governmental loans to the Allies was contracted *after* the close of hostilities, but their bargaining potentialities were not exploited.

Wilson's conception of a just peace demanded that the United States play an independent and leading role. But his conception that a durable peace also depended upon an Allied victory bound him to the Allied powers with economic and moral sinews. It was inconceivable to go to the Peace Conference only to risk a breach with one's former allies by taking the part of the defeated powers. A statesman who looks forward to a peaceful world based upon international co-operation will not drive a hard bargain with the very nations upon whose collaboration he feels most dependent. Wilson might force Clemenceau and Lloyd George to accept the Fourteen Points as the theoretical basis of the peace, but once the talks began, the dynamics of the situation delivered him into their hands, for his very hopes and ideals tended to paralyze him as a negotiator. At Paris he realized the prophetic truth of his own words to Frank Cobb: the war *had* overthrown peacetime standards and values, and not even Woodrow Wilson was left to uphold them. "Only a peace between equals can last," he had said, but the peace that ensued was a peace between masters and slaves, and the President of the United States found himself holding a whip with the others. "It is a very severe settlement with Germany," he affirmed in September 1919, "but there is not anything in it that she did not earn."

The program Wilson took to Paris envisioned a world order based upon national self-determination, free trade, and a League of Nations to keep the peace. "What we seek," he explained, "is the reign of law, based upon the consent of the governed and sustained by the organized opinion of mankind." National self-determination, the international equivalent of democracy in domestic politics, would embody the principle of consent of the governed. Free trade would soften national rivalries and broaden prosperity. The League was to give security to the whole system through mutual guarantees of territorial integrity and common action against an aggressor.

Conspicuously absent from the Fourteen Points was any meaningful demand for a substantial change in international economic relations. Eight of the Fourteen Points applied the doctrine of self-determination to specific parts of Europe. The remaining six points were of general application, and of these only three dealt with economic matters: freedom of the seas in peace and in war, the removal of all economic barriers between nations, and an impartial adjustment of colonial claims. Not one of these three points represented anything more than a pious hope, and not one was even remotely realized in fact. The structure of colonial claims was hardly touched by the mandate system of the League. Freedom of the seas had to be waived at the outset upon the insistence of the British, who would not even indulge in the hypocrisy of endorsing it on principle. The removal of economic barriers was an idle suggestion if one could not remove the economic and social structures, the profit motives and systems of domestic business power that made trade barriers inevitable; Wilson dared not even try to commit his own country to further removal of trade barriers—and it was the United States that actually began international tariff warfare in the postwar era. Finally, the idea of multiplying national sovereignties and expecting a reduction of international trade barriers to follow was certainly tempting the wrath of the gods.

The peace that was signed at Versailles was a political peace in which the fundamental economic arrangements of nineteenth-century Europe were taken for granted. Wilson himself told his commission of American experts that he was "not much interested in the economic subjects" that might be discussed at Paris; and John Maynard Keynes has remarked that "the fundamental economic problems of a Europe starving and disintegrating before their eyes was the one question in which it was impossible to arouse the interest of the Four." Thorstein Veblen wrote in 1919 that the Covenant of the League

is a political document, an instrument of *Realpolitik*, created in the image of nineteenth century imperialism. It has been set up by political statesmen, on political grounds, for political ends, and with political apparatus to be used with political effects. . . . True to the political tradition, the Covenant provides for enforcing the peace by recourse to arms and commercial hostilities, but it contemplates no measures for avoiding war by avoiding the status quo out of which the great war arose.

Wilson, in short, failed again to grapple with economics, as he had failed to grapple with it in the political theory of his academic years. During his career in practical politics he had learned to mold his appeal along the lines of group and class interests and to resolve political conflicts into economic issues, but somehow when he stepped into the world theater he lapsed once again into the intellectual primness and gentility of the old-fashioned professor who had been enthralled with what he thought was the disinterestedness of the great British statesmen, and who had said of the American Senate in the Gilded Age that it was "divorced from class interests." The end of his career was full of contradictions, in which the Wilson of *Congressional Government* struggled with the Wilson who had acquired a more mature and realistic education in American party battles. What he said about the causes of the war had little relation to the manner in which he made the peace.

In an address on September 27, 1918 he had declared:

Special alliances and economic rivalries and hostilities have been the prolific source in the modern world of the plans and passions that produce war. It would be an insincere as well as insecure peace that did not exclude them in definite and binding terms.

Having made just such an insecure peace, he returned to the United States to defend it, and in the course of his defense said again at St. Louis, September 5, 1919:

Why, my fellow citizens, is there any man here or any woman, let me say is there any child here, who does not know that the seed of war in the modern world is industrial and commercial rivalry? The real reason that the war that we have just finished took place was that Germany was afraid her commercial rivals were going to get the better of her, and the reason why some nations went into the war against Germany was that they thought Germany would get the commercial advantage of them . . . This war, in its inception, was a commercial and industrial war. It was not a political war.

No wonder, then, that Wilson's League, which was not intended or designed to change the system of commercial and industrial rivalries, was inadequate to prevent war. Europe, desperately in need of economic unity under large-scale industrial technology, was partitioned into an increased number of economically unstable and strategically indefensible small states. Germany, the economic hub of the Continent, was crippled in so far as Britain and France found it in their power to do. This disorganized and broken world of competing nationalist enterprises the League was expected to preserve and make secure. The League itself did not represent a vital change, but simply an attempt to give organization to the old chaos.

No matter how historians may dramatize Wilson's struggle with Clemenceau and Lloyd George, it was not a struggle between an Old Order and a New Order, but merely a quarrel as to how the Old Order should settle its affairs. In this attempt to organize and regulate a failing system of competitive forces the theme of Wilson's domestic leadership was repeated on a world scale. Just as the New Freedom had been, under the idealistic form of a crusade for the rights and opportunities of the small man, an

effort to restore the archaic conditions of nineteenth-century competition, so the Treaty and the League Covenant were an attempt, in the language of democracy, peace, and self-determination, to retain the competitive national state system of the nineteenth century without removing the admitted source of its rivalries and animosities. It had always been Wilson's aim to preserve the essentials of the *status quo* by reforming it; but failing essentially to reform, he was unable in the end to preserve.

In March 1919 Wilson's old friend of the New Jersey period, George L. Record, who had played a large part in converting him to progressivism, sent him a remarkable letter, analyzing the inadequacy of Wilson's conceptions to the present era. Wilson, Record wrote frankly, had

ignored the great issue which is slowly coming to the front, the question of economic democracy, abolition of privilege, and securing to men the full fruits of their labor or service.

There is no glory . . . in standing for the principles of political democracy . . . [which] is like standing for the Ten Commandments . . .

The issue of political democracy has passed. The issue is now one of industrial or economic democracy.

The League of Nations idea will not help your position, either now or in history, because, like all your other policies, it does not go to the root of the problem. Wars are caused by privilege. Every modern state is governed by the privileged, that is, by those who control industry by owning railroads, lands, mines, banks, and credit. These men thus obtain enormous and unearned capital, for which there is no use in the country where it is produced, because the poverty of the workers limits the home market. Those who control this surplus capital must seek new countries and new people to exploit, and this clash of selfish interests leads to war. The cure for war is the reign of justice, i.e., the abolition of privilege in each of the great nations. I do not believe that you can set up machinery which will maintain justice in international relations among governments which deny justice to their own people. If the League works, it will be when and to the extent that justice is established by the present governments of the Allies; if it has any real power, it is very likely to be used as an international bulwark of privilege. That danger looms large after you pass off the scene . . .

Record urged Wilson to supplement his international program with a social-democratic program at home, including a demand for public-utility ownership and limitation of great fortunes. It might be impossible to realize this program, he admitted, but Wilson's failure would be only temporary. Future generations would recognize his wisdom and acclaim him "a truly great man."

Wilson acknowledged Record's letter cordially. Almost a year before receiving it he had expressed somewhat similar sentiments to Professor Axson. The two were talking about the qualifications of the next President, and Wilson remarked that he must be a philosophical man, capable of thinking in world terms. At present, "the only really internationally minded people are the labor people."

The world is going to change radically, and I am satisfied that governments will have to do many things which are now left to individuals and corporations. I am satisfied for instance that the government will have to take over all the great natural resources . . . all the water power, all the coal mines, all the oil fields, etc. They will have to be government-owned.

If I should say that outside, people would call me a socialist, but I am not a socialist. And it is because I am not a socialist that

I believe these things. I think the only way we can prevent communism is by some such action as that . . .

But if Wilson's private convictions were really evolving from American progressivism to an international social-democratic point of view, the fact is not registered in his public policies. The last part of his career seems like the work of a somnambulist who repeats unerringly his appointed workday rounds while his mind moves in an insulated shadow world. If he believed his fine statements with the depth and emphasis with which he made them, he may well have accounted his career as a world statesman a series of failures. He appealed for neutrality in thought and deed, and launched upon a diplomatic policy that is classic for its partisanship. He said that American entrance into the war would be a world calamity, and led the nation in. He said that only a peace between equals would last, and participated in the *Diktat* of Versailles. He said that the future security of the world depended on removing the economic causes of war, and did not attempt even to discuss these causes at the Peace Conference. He declared his belief in the future of government ownership, and allowed his administration to close in a riot of reaction. He wanted desperately to bring the United States into the League, and launched on a course of action that made American participation impossible. No wonder that in one of his moments of apprehension he should have confessed to George Creel: "What I seem to see—with all my heart I hope that I am wrong—is a tragedy of disappointment."

And yet it is his hopes and promises that make Wilson's record seem so bleak. Set against the dark realities, it is defensible. In the Fourteen Points he produced a more sane and liberal, if not enduring, basis for peace than anyone else among the belligerents. By appealing to the hopes of Germany he helped to bring an earlier armistice. Harsh as the treaty was, it would have been materially worse without his influence. He went to Europe handicapped by his apparent repudiation in the Congressional elections of 1918, limited by the national claims and secret treaties of his allies, tied to the technique of compromise by his hopes for the League, committed by his belief in capitalism and nationalism to accept the major consequences of the disaster they had wrought. Confronted time and time again at Paris with a series of insoluble dilemmas, faced with too many battles on too many fronts, he became, in Charles Seymour's words, "the plaything of events." Granting the severe limitations imposed upon his work by the logic of the situation, Paul Birdsall, in his *Versailles Twenty Years After,* finds "an extraordinary consistency in Wilson's fight for his program under overwhelming difficulties, as well as a high degree of political intelligence in translating the abstract principles of his

program into concrete details of application."

Clemenceau habitually dozed off when matters unrelated to French security were under consideration at the Conference. Lloyd George on more than one occasion admitted lightheartedly his ignorance of some of the most elementary facts of European economics and geography. ("Please refresh my memory," he once asked an aide. "Is it Upper or Lower Silesia that we are giving away?") Wilson begged his experts: "Tell me what is right and I will fight for it. Give me a guaranteed position," and went down on hands and knees in his suite until the small hours of the mornings, poring over maps and charts, trying to master the complicated maze of fact involved in the negotiations. Although he felt obliged to defend the peace in the United States, sometimes in incredible language—"a people's treaty," "the great humane document of all time"—he well knew how vulnerable it was. His remark that the much-criticized Shantung settlement was the best that could be salvaged from "a dirty past" might well have been his verdict on the treaty as a whole. . . .

Etienne Mantoux: A REPLY TO KEYNES

"It was to the coming generation that Mr. Keynes dedicated his book twenty-five years ago. This is an answer which comes from that generation." Shortly after inscribing this conclusion to his manuscript and scarcely a week before the war ended, Etienne Mantoux was killed in action fighting with French forces against Hitler's retreating armies. His father had been present as official interpreter at the most secret sessions of the Big Four in 1919. He himself had traveled widely in Europe and America, done graduate work at the London School of Economics, and been on intimate terms with leading intellectual figures before the war. No one in his generation could claim better qualifications for the task of re-examining Keynes's verdict on the Treaty of Versailles. And for this youthful Frenchman that seemed an urgently necessary task in 1941 when he undertook it. "To examine Mr. Keynes's pronouncements over the last Peace," wrote Mantoux, "is neither to rake up old grievances nor to disinter dead issues; the issue is nothing else than what the coming Peace is to be."

*T*HE *Economic Consequences of the Peace* appeared in the United States in January 1920. It had a phenomenal sale. "The truth is," said General Smuts many years later, "America wanted a reason for denying Wilson. The world wanted a scapegoat. At that opportune moment Keynes brought out his *Economic Consequences of the Peace*. There were a few pages about Wilson in it which exactly suited the policies of America and the world's mood. When I encouraged Keynes to write that book, I knew his views about the statesmen at Paris. But I did not expect a personal note in his book. I did not expect him to turn Wilson into a figure of fun. These few pages about Wilson in Keynes's book made an Aunt Sally of the noblest figure—perhaps the only noble figure—in the history of the war, and they led a fashion against Wilson that was adopted by the Intelligentsia of the day and is not yet past— the Intelligentsia (not the Intellectuals)

—the people who, admiring only their own cleverness, despise real goodness, real thought, real wisdom. . . . Every paper I saw," added the General, "quoted the part about Wilson's bamboozlement. Wilson was already going down in America. In their hearts, the Americans wanted him to go down: they wanted to evade the duties he imposed on them. The book was absolutely to their purpose. It helped to finish Wilson, and it strengthened the Americans against the League."

Judging from the use made of Mr. Keynes's book during the debate over the Peace Treaty, it is hard to find fault with General Smuts's comments. The book was seized by the President's opponents as a first-rate weapon in the fight then raging. It was quoted extensively as evidence of the infamous deeds committed at Paris, and in which America would not connive. On 10 February, Senator Borah read long extracts in the

From Etienne Mantoux, *The Carthaginian Peace or the Economic Consequences of Mr. Keynes*, pp. 9–11, 186–188. Reprinted by permission.

Senate; his comments could scarcely improve upon Mr. Keynes's text.

"His contention," he said, "is that the German Treaty consigns continental Europe to perpetual famine and chronic revolution; that unless the Treaty is completely revised and rewritten, it must inevitably result that the economic system of Europe will be destroyed, which will result in the loss of millions of lives and in revolution after revolution, which necessarily follows when a people find themselves in the condition to which the people of Europe will be reduced. . . . When you think of the fact that they have lightly wrecked the entire economic system of an entire continent and reduced to starvation millions of people and perhaps prevented the world peace from coming at all in this decade, there is no language too severe for such men. . . . The Treaty in its consequences is a crime born of blind revenge and insatiable greed."

One month later, the Treaty was finally defeated. From that time on, the Keynesian picture was to remain implanted in the American mind. The horrors of Versailles became a veritable article of faith. They were used at every juncture to show that there was really no difference between the nations of Europe—that they were all equally revengeful, equally Machiavellian, equally imperialistic; that the entry of America in the last war had been a ghastly mistake; and that the issue of any new one would be to her a matter of indifference, for an Allied victory would probably be no better than Versailles and a German victory could certainly be no worse. And thus, in sheer despair of a continent that would not be redeemed, America declared herself neutral: should war break out, she would be interested in neither party; all she would be interested in was

keeping out. Whatever might happen in Europe, it was all the fault of Versailles.

* * *

In *The Economic Consequences of the Peace*, Mr. Keynes predicted that the Treaty, if it was carried into effect, "must impair yet further, when it might have restored, the delicate, complicated organisation, already shaken and broken by war, through which alone the European peoples can employ themselves and live." Europe would be threatened with "a long, silent process of semi-starvation, and of a gradual, steady lowering of the standards of life and comfort." Ten years after the Treaty, European production was well above its prewar level, and European standards of living had never been higher.

He predicted that the iron output of Europe would decline as a consequence of the Treaty. In the ten years that followed the Treaty, the iron output of Europe, which had fallen considerably during the War, increased almost continuously. In 1919, Europe produced 10 per cent more iron than in the record year 1913, and would no doubt have produced still more had not the producers combined to restrict output for fear of injuring prices by overproduction.

He predicted that the iron and steel output of Germany would diminish. By 1927, Germany produced nearly 30 per cent more iron and 38 per cent more steel than in the record year 1913, within the same territorial limits.

He predicted that the efficiency of the German coal-mining industry, lowered by the War, would remain low as a consequence of the peace. By 1925, the efficiency of labour, which had dropped seriously in the meantime, was already higher, in the Ruhr coal industries, than in 1913; in 1927 it was higher by nearly

20 per cent; and in 1929 by more than 30 per cent.

He predicted that a pre-war level of output could not be expected in the German coal industry. In 1920, 1921, and 1922, coal output was well above the average level of the five years preceding the war, within the same territorial limits. It fell sharply in 1923, and was slightly below pre-war average in 1924. It was above that average in 1925; and in 1926, it was already higher than in the record year 1913.

He predicted that Germany "cannot export coal in the near future, . . . if she is to continue as an industrial nation." In the first year following the Treaty, Germany exported (net) 15 million tons of coal; and in 1926 she exported (net) 35 million tons, or *twice* the amount of the average (1909–13) pre-war exports of *all* her pre-war territories.

He predicted that the German mercantile marine "cannot be restored for many years to come on a scale adequate to meet the requirements of her own commerce." The total German tonnage was a little above 5 millions in 1913. It was reduced in 1920 to 673,000; but in 1924 it already approached 3 million tons; in 1930 it was well above 4 million, and German liners were the wonder of the transatlantic world.

He predicted that "after what she has uffered in the war and by the Peace," Germany's annual savings would "fall 'ar short of what they were before." The monthly increase in German savings bank deposits was 84 million in 1913; in 1925 it had become 13 million; and in 1928 it was nearly 210 million.

He predicted that Germany's annual surplus would be reduced to less than 2 milliard marks. In 1925, the net accumulation of domestic capital was esti-mated at 6.4 milliards, and in 1927 at 7.6 milliards.

He predicted that in the next thirty years, Germany could not possibly be expected to pay more than 2 milliard marks a year in reparation. In the six years preceding September 1939, Germany, by Hitler's showing, had spent each year on rearmament alone about seven times as much.

*   *   *

But was not just this, it will be said, the very danger against which Mr. Keynes had warned us? Was not National Socialism a product of the years of destitution, aggravated by the ravages of the Great Depression, all of which were the consequences of Versailles?

The figures I have given to illustrate the economic recovery of Germany after the Treaty cover a period of ten years; that much, I submit, is enough to satisfy anybody that the Treaty that was to destroy the economic organization of Europe did not in fact have this effect, and did not even prevent economic activity from recovering to levels that were often higher than before 1914, in spite of all the havoc caused by four years of uninterrupted warfare. After 1929, this process was reversed and economic activity fell sharply throughout the whole world. Was this, then, the tidal wave of 1919?

That economic nationalism, with its clumsy resort to state control, to trade restriction, and to currency manipulation was a serious aggravating factor, is hardly open to doubt. It was not, of course, confined to Europe only. But in so far as the Treaties of 1919 had allowed the forces of nationalism to consolidate a structure of autonomous states in Central Europe, they probably contributed in some degree to the severity of the depression, at least in that part of the world. This aspect of the Treaties of 1919, however, although it was referred to several times, was not one of the essential points of Mr. Keynes's analysis, which was concerned with the Treaty of Versailles and the treatment of Germany rather than with the settlement of Central and Eastern Europe. But what is more important, the dangers which were, in his view, to follow from the treaty did not lie precisely in this direction. What he had feared in 1919, as a consequence of the alleged disorganization of the European economy, was a lasting and widespread *diminution* of production; but the crisis of 1929 was one of *over-production*—at least, of relative over-production. Whatever may have been the true causes of this highly complex phenomenon, it is surely a rather simplified solution to refer it back to the Treaty of Versailles. What would be needed is an explanation of how precisely the Treaty was responsible for the cyclical depression of the 'thirties. I have not so far encountered one—not, at any rate, in the writings which Mr. Keynes himself has devoted, in later years, to this vexing problem. If the Great Depression was really a consequence of the peace, it certainly was not one that Mr. Keynes (or anyone else, for that matter) had ever led us to expect.

An inquiry into the nature of the economic disasters following from the Treaty does not, therefore, lead us very far, or else it leads us too far. No doubt not all was rosy in Europe during the post-war decade, and economic recovery was not immediate; after four years of unprecedented destruction and disintegration, nobody could have expected it to be. The wearing out of capital equipment, the breakdown of transport, the

hypertrophy of national debts and the resulting inflation of the currency—and, above all, the uprooting of millions of human lives—all these were the legacy of War, not of the Treaty. Nor was it explained how the Treaty was to aggravate them. "It will no longer," wrote Mr. Keynes in his chapter on "Europe after the Treaty," "be part of my purpose to distinguish between the inevitable fruits of the War and the avoidable misfortunes of the Peace."

Why, then, speak of the Economic Consequences of the *Peace?* We have seen either that most of the threatened consequences did not occur, or that those which occurred were due to other causes, and were therefore not predicted. Yet the impression has almost universally persisted that the economic evils which afflicted Europe in the post-war decades must be imputed to the Treaty. "It is hard," wrote Allyn Young, "to be patient with men who point to the economic dissolution war has wrought and say: 'There are the fruits of your peace.'"

But still, some will insist, is it possible to deny that Hitler was the product of Versailles? And even if the German people was not reduced to actual starvation, was it not driven into despair? And would not a more generous attitude on the part of the Allies have prevented the rise of National Socialism?

Whether or not a policy of complete forgetfulness would have succeeded in appeasing Germany from the outset will, of course, never be known. What *is* known, on the other hand, is the policy that *was* followed up to the time of the National Socialist Revolution, and the march of events that accompanied it.

After the partial failure of M. Poincaré's policy of "coercion" in the Ruhr, the Dawes Plan inaugurated, as we have seen, a new phase in Reparation policy, placing upon Germany the most moderate demands, and assisting their execution with an initial loan. In 1924 the French Army evacuated the Ruhr. Less than one year later, Marshal Hindenburg was elected President of the Reich by a coalition of nationalists.

In 1930 the Young Plan was adopted as a final settlement of Reparations, involving a very considerable reduction of Germany's burden. At the same time, the French Army evacuated the Rhineland, five years in advance of the Treaty's original time-limit. Less than three months later, the National Socialist party, until then relatively insignificant, polled 6,400,000 votes out of a total of 35,000,000 and obtained 107 seats in the Reichstag.

In the summer of 1931 Reparation payments were suspended. The following year, Hitler polled 13,400,000 votes against 19,300,000 to Marshal Hindenburg in the Presidential election.

On 9 July 1932 all Reparations were finally abolished at the Conference of Lausanne. On 21 July, Hitler's party obtained 13,700,000 votes and 230 seats at the general election, thus becoming the strongest in the Reichstag.

The disarmament clauses of the Treaty had proved among the sorest to Germany's national pride. In December 1932 equality of rights was conceded to Germany at the Disarmament Conference in a declaration to which the German Government gave its adhesion. Less than two months later, Hitler was called by Marshal Hindenburg to be Chancellor of the Reich.

*   *   *

Albert Thomas, the late Director of the International Labour Office, is reported to have asked Mr. Henry Ford once what he thought of the Russian problem. "There isn't any," was the reply. "In the last six months I delivered 275,000 dollars' worth of tractors to Russia and got paid every cent."

If, as is sometimes suggested to-day, we are to take this ingenuous view of the various "problems" of the world, their solution ought not to be unduly difficult. It would be difficult, rather, to understand why they have not all been solved long ago. It is a particularly widespread fashion to insist that since economic needs must take precedence over older fashioned political and national traditions, since the troubles of Europe are mostly economic in origin, the constitution in Europe of "large units" where mass production would not be impeded by restrictions between its areas should be our predominant aim. Thus, as Professor E. H. Carr has explained, "Naumann with his *Mittel-Europa* proved a surer prophet than Wilson with his principle of self-determination." But then, it may be added, Hitler proved an even better one than either of these; for if the aim of welding Europe into one single economic whole were really to outweigh all others, then the war waged for over five years at such a cost of life and treasure, against the "integration" of Europe under Germany, would be not only criminal but insane.

It is not inconceivable that a day may come when the world will be brought under the rule of the single planetary empire. Until then mankind will continue to be divided into separate nations, or groups of nations, and the "problem," in the meantime, will not be to establish a peace that may always easily be obtained by acquiescence in the will of the strongest, but to maintain as long as possible such conditions as will give to the freedom of each its legitimate due. "Large units," in this respect, will be conducive to peace and freedom, not by any inherent virtue, but in proportion to circumstances only—to their internal composition and to the relation towards their neighbours big or small—and these in turn will be found to be usually a product of *geographical* circumstance. "Large units" and economic prosperity have not been wholly unknown in the past; yet the blessings that have followed have not been unmixed. In 1914, full in an era of economic prosperity unprecedented in the annals of mankind, "large units" proved a very meagre foundation for the peace of Europe. To use an argument about the economic "Balkanization" of Central and South-Eastern Europe after 1919 as an explanation of the breakdown is therefore a little short of the mark.

Now, the present book was never intended as an apologia for the Treaty of Versailles; but while the economic defects of that settlement were, for the most part, illusory or exaggerated, the present writer shares the opinion of those who have maintained that the political defects were the really decisive ones. It may have been a mistake, from the economic point of view, to allow or even encourage the break-up of the Danubian Monarchy into several sovereign states; but these states were always free, had they found it to their interest, to organize themselves into some sort of economic federation, and in so far as they failed to do this, the economic loss thus caused has been sustained primarily by themselves. How much more serious to the rest of the world, on the other hand, have been the *political* consequences of the division of Central and South-Eastern Europe! There, as has in fact frequently been pointed out, lay the cardinal vice of the system—in the constitution of a Europe where a strong

and centralized Germany of some 70 millions remained surrounded by a string of small states, who had to rely for the preservation of their independence upon the assistance of faraway powers; to put it shortly, in the failure, and one might almost say in the deliberate failure, to establish a true *balance of power.* For Wilson himself, intent though he was upon the rejection of this type of diplomatic system, had foreseen that the Europe which he had thus left, largely by his own doing, was not one that could be expected to stand by itself—that without the support of *outside* Powers, Germany would yet have her will upon it. "All the nations that Germany meant to crush and reduce to the status of tools in her own hands have been redeemed by this war," he had explained, "and given the guarantee of the strongest nations of the world that nobody shall invade their liberty again. If you do not want to give them that guarantee, then you make it certain that . . . the attempt will be made again, and if another war starts like this one, are you going to keep out of it?" Now, the League of Nations was designed to ensure precisely this kind of support. But the powers concerned proved themselves unwilling, undecided, or unprepared to face their responsibilities in time. The truth is, that the spirit in which the League had been conceived presumed too much of them. As has been well said, "it was not the League that failed, but the nations." And if Wilson was guilty of one illusion, that illusion was mankind.

"If," said the President, "this treaty should be refused, if it should be impaired, then amidst the tragedy of the things that would follow every man would be converted to the opinion that I am now uttering, but," he added, "I do not want to see that sort of conversion. I do not want to see an era of blood and chaos to convert men to the only practical methods of justice." Is it conceivable that we should rest our hopes again upon some renovated scheme of mutual assistance? Such systems may look well on paper; but paper, as Catherine of Russia said, is not so ticklish as the human skin—and this is the raw material supplied in the last resort to the ingenuity of statesmen. When the time comes to build again a world organization, they will do well to take care to reckon, as Sir Halford Mackinder had warned them twenty-five years ago, with "realities"—not merely with economic realities, but with physical and geographical, with human and with political realities; in their calculations, the size of continents, the width of seas, the shape of coastlines, the position of rivers, mountains, plains and deserts, of islands, canals and straits—and, above all, of the numbers and character of peoples, must enter as much as the figures for wheat, coal, of petroleum output; their first task, before they can lay down the durable foundations of world organization, will be to consider the materials out of which it is to be built. . . .

Walter Lippmann:
MIRAGES OF WILSON'S FOREIGN POLICY

In 1919 Walter Lippmann ardently supported the Wilsonian peace program. He helped to prepare an important memorandum explaining to the Allies what each of the Fourteen Points meant. Under Colonel House's direction he worked for Wilson at Paris. But when in 1943 Lippmann published his views on past and present requirements for American foreign policy, the following passages indicated a clear revision in his estimate of Wilson. Lippmann was well aware of this and other departures from his previous opinions. In a preface he explained that the conclusions set down here had been the product of long experience: "I have come to them slowly over thirty years, and as a result of many false starts, mistaken judgments, and serious disappointments."

THE occasion for going to war was Germany's unrestricted use of the submarine against American merchant shipping on the Atlantic routes from North America to the British Isles and France. But the substantial and compelling reason for going to war was that the cutting of the Atlantic communications meant the starvation of Britain and, therefore, the conquest of Western Europe by imperial Germany.

President Wilson avoided this explanation of his decision to intervene, choosing instead to base his decision upon the specific legal objection to unrestricted submarine warfare and upon a generalized moral objection to lawless and cruel aggression. But these superfi-

From *U. S. Foreign Policy*, by Walter Lippmann, pp. 33–39, 71–77. By permission of Little, Brown and Co. and The Atlantic Monthly Press. Copyright 1943 by Walter Lippmann.

cial reasons for the declaration of war would never have carried the day if a majority of the people had not recognized intuitively, and if some Americans had not seen clearly, what the threatened German victory would mean to the United States. Though there was lacking the tradition of a foreign policy which made the matter self-evident, many Americans saw in 1917 that if Germany won, the United States would have to face a new and aggressively expanding German empire which had made Britain, France, and Russia its vassals, and Japan its ally. They saw that in such a position the defense of the Western Hemisphere would require immense armaments over and above those needed in the Pacific, and that America would have to live in a perpetual state of high and alert military preparedness. It was in this very concrete and practical sense, though unhappily President Wilson preferred not to particularize, that a German victory in 1917 would have made the world unsafe for the American democracies from Canada to the Argentine.

This in brief was the undeclared, and only partially realized, foreign policy which determined the participation of the United States in the first German World War. The sinking of merchant ships without visit and search, and without provision for the safety of crews and passengers, would not in itself have been the *casus belli* if the German submarines had caused less destruction. Sporadic sinkings would have continued to lead to protests, as they did in 1915 and 1916, and probably to reprisals. But they would not have led to war if by 1917 the submarine had not become so destructive as to make it seem probable that Germany would starve out Britain and isolate France.

Nor did the United States go to war to make the world safe for all democracies: if it had seemed probable that Germany would be defeated by czarist Russia, the United States would have remained neutral because its vital interests in the North Atlantic would have remained secure. The war was certainly not engaged to overthrow the Kaiser and to make Germany a democratic republic: if the Germans had not broken into the Atlantic and threatened the whole structure of our Atlantic defenses, private citizens would still have made faces at the Kaiser, but the nation would not have made war upon him.

The United States did not go to war because it wished to found a League of Nations; it went to war in order to preserve American security. And when the war was over, the nation would almost certainly have accepted in some form or other the scheme of the League of Nations if President Wilson had been able to demonstrate to the people that the League would perpetuate the security which the military victory had won for them. Mr. Wilson failed to make this demonstration. He failed because in leading the nation to war he had failed to give the durable and compelling reasons for the momentous decision. The reasons he did give were legalistic and moralistic and idealistic reasons, rather than the substantial and vital reason that the security of the United States demanded that no aggressively expanding imperial power, like Germany, should be allowed to gain the mastery of the Atlantic Ocean.

Because this simple and self-evident American interest was not candidly made explicit, the nation never understood clearly why it had entered the war. As time went on, the country was, therefore, open to every suggestion and insinuation that the nation had fought for no good reason at all, that its victory was meaningless, that it had been maneuvered into a non-American war by the international bankers and the British diplomats. And so, having failed to make plain that the war was waged for a vital American interest, President Wilson had no way of proving to the nation that his settlement of the war really concerned the United States. The war had been fought without a foreign policy, and neither President Wilson nor the nation had the means, therefore, of judging whether the League was merely a foreign, or was also an American, interest.

Thus the longer the Senate debated the Treaty of Versailles with its covenant, the more the people felt that there was no compelling connection between their vital interests and the program which President Wilson offered them. They saw that the League imposed upon the United States the unprecedented commitment to help enforce the peace of Europe. They saw only what they were asked to contribute. For they had not been taught to understand what British and French power meant to the security of America's vital interests all over the world.

They had not had it demonstrated to them how much the defense of the Western Hemisphere depended upon having friendly and strong partners in the British Isles, in the French ports on the Atlantic, at Gibraltar and Casablanca and Dakar; or how much the defense of the Philippines depended upon French Indo-China, and upon British Hong Kong, Malaya, and Burma, and upon the attitude and the strength of Russia and upon China in Eastern Asia. The legalistic, moralistic, idealistic presentation of the war and of the League obscured the realities—caused it to appear that for

what we were asked to give to our allies, we were to receive nothing from them. It was made to seem that the new responsibilities of the League flowed from President Wilson's philanthropy and not from the vital necessity of finding allies to support America's vast existing commitments in the Western Hemisphere and all the way across the Pacific to the China coast.

Not until twenty years later, not until France had fallen and Britain was in mortal peril, not until the Japanese had surrounded the Philippines, did it become possible for the nation to perceive the hidden but real structure of America's strategic position in the world. . . .

When the prejudice against alliances encountered the desire to abolish war, the result was the Wilsonian conception of collective security. As Wilson saw it, the cause of the first World War was the system of alliances which had divided Europe into the Triple Alliance and the Triple Entente, and in his mind it was necessary to liquidate alliances in order to organize peace through the League of Nations. Articles 23, 24, 25 were written into the Covenant by President Wilson in order to liquidate old alliances and prevent the formation of new ones. Thus collective security was to be the remedy and the substitute for alliances.

There was a negligible minority at the time who did not share this, the Wilsonian view, but held that a system of collective security could not be maintained unless within it there existed an alliance of strong and dependable powers. They held that a nucleus of leading states, allied for the defense of their vital interests, was needed in order to enforce peace through a system of collective security.

Wilson, however, not only shared the traditional prejudices against alliances but was deeply influenced also by the idea that the nations could be brought together by consent, as the thirteen American colonies had been brought together first in a confederation and then in a federal union. This analogy has long been cherished by Americans as affording the hope that it might become a model for the rest of the world.

Yet it is, I submit, a profoundly misleading analogy. For the thirteen colonies had been planted and had matured under one sovereign power, that of the English crown. They had fought the War of Independence under the government of a Continental Congress which resolved to draw up Articles of Confederation even before the Battle of Bunker Hill, which adopted the Articles in 1777, and saw them ratified and in force before Cornwallis surrendered at Yorktown. The former colonies remained a confederation after the war was over, and when they adopted the present Constitution they were, as they themselves insisted, forming "a more perfect union."

They were not forming an altogether unprecedented union; they were perpetuating and perfecting a union which had always existed since the plantation of the British colonies. The fact that none of the Spanish or French colonies joined the union is fairly conclusive evidence that even in North America—three thousand miles from Europe—political unions do not become comprehensive by voluntary consent.

If the historic experience of Britain, France, Russia, Germany, and Italy is a guide, it tells us that the large states have grown up around the nucleus of a strong principality—England, the Ile de France, Muscovy, Piedmont, Prussia. By conquest, by royal marriages, by providing protection to weaker principalities, by the gravitation of the smaller to the bigger, the large national unions were gradually pulled together.

President Wilson's conception of collective security did not take into account this historic pattern. He held that there should be a union of fifty juridically equal but otherwise unequal states, and not the evolution of a union from a nucleus of firmly allied strong states. Refusing to regard alliances as the effective means by which collective security could be made to operate, Wilson forbade the founders of the League of Nations to perfect their alliance which had been tested in the fires of war. He did, to be sure, reluctantly agree to the French demand for a special guarantee in return for France's giving up the Rhine frontier. But he regarded this as a compromise of his principles and readily abandoned it.

Wilson identified collective security with antipathy to alliances, rather than with the constructive development of alliances. The influence of this idea played a great part in dividing the Americans from the British and the French, and the British from the French. For the French saw from the first, being closer to the realities of Europe, that the League could enforce the peace only if the League were led by a strong combination of powers resolved to enforce the peace. The French, therefore, sought allies in Europe, all the more urgently as they saw their alliance with Britain dissolving. This alienated the British, who believed in the Wilsonian League, and pushed them toward encouraging the German revolt against the settlement.

Then, as time went on, the League became impotent because the nuclear alliance of Britain, France, and America had been dissolved. Above all, the League was impotent to prevent our present enemies from forming their Tripartite Pact. Twenty years after the League was founded, the great military alliance of Germany, Italy, and Japan had been formed. But the generalized, abstract system of collective security had fallen to pieces.

It will be said that the Wilsonian ideal could have been realized if the Senate had not refused to ratify the Treaty of Versailles. Perhaps so. But if it had been realized, the League would, I submit, have succeeded, because American participation would in practice have been tantamount to a working nuclear alliance—in Monroe's phrase to "a concert by agreement"—with Great Britain primarily, and with France indirectly. This alliance has had to be reconstructed in order to conduct the present war. If it had existed after 1919, and had been perfected, it might have prevented the present war. Certainly it would at least have prevented Britain and America from disarming one another in the presence of Japan and Germany. And if the war had come nevertheless, we should not have been brought so perilously near to disaster.

The American opponents of the League saw truly that if the League was actually going to enforce peace, then it must imply the equivalent of an Anglo-American alliance. If the League did not imply that, then the generalized commitments of the Covenant were too broad and too unpredictable to be intelligible. Thus Wilson was placed in a dilemma: if the League was a practical instrument, it contained an alliance, and all good and true men including Wilson were opposed to any idea of an alliance; if in fact the League outlawed alliances, and still sought to enforce peace, then it was an unlimited commitment supported by no clear means of fulfilling it. Thus the League was attacked both as

a concealed alliance in the realm of power politics and as a utopian pipe dream.

The dilemma was presented because Wilson was trying to establish collective security without forming an alliance. He wanted the omelet. He rejected the idea of cooking the eggs. The people, agreeing that an alliance was abhorrent, proceeded by intuitive common sense to the conviction that without an alliance, the League was unworkable and unpredictably dangerous.

Thus in the debacle of Wilson's proposals we see the culminating effect of the American misunderstanding of alliances. Wilson as well as the men who opposed him had carried over into the twentieth century the illusion fostered in the nineteenth century—that the United States had never had allies and that the purest American tradition was opposed to alliances. The concert with Britain, which Monroe, Jefferson, and Madison had established in 1823, had been the foundation of American foreign relations for seventy-five years. But though it existed in fact, it had never been avowed as a policy.

Thus in the fateful period from 1898 to 1941 the United States engaged in three wars but never succeeded in forming a foreign policy. We could have had a foreign policy only by agreeing that since our commitments had been extended, a concert by agreement had to be extended correspondingly. But the modes of thought which Washington, Jefferson, and Madison had as a matter of course used had been forgotten through disuse. Thus the nation was unable to form any foreign policy after the war with Spain, or after the first World War. And as yet it has not been able to form a policy in the second World War. . . .

George F. Kennan: AMERICAN DIPLOMACY

George F. Kennan had spent twenty-five years as a career diplomat when in 1950 he wrote the book from which these excerpts are taken. He had been Director of the Policy Planning Staff in the State Department, author of an influential article expounding the "containment" policy for dealing with Russia, and he was about to be appointed Ambassador to Russia. Having noticed "the lack of an adequately stated and widely accepted theoretical foundation to underpin the conduct of our external relations," he turned to the history of American foreign policy over the last half-century with several questions in mind. What concepts had animated our statesmen in their diplomatic efforts? What did they feel they were trying to achieve? "And were these concepts, in the light of retrospect, appropriate and effective ones?" Kennan's generally negative conclusions on this last question did much to provoke the debate over "realism" versus "idealism" as foundations for our foreign policy.

WORLD WAR I

WE have now come, in the course of this undertaking, to what seems to me the most baffling, most tragic, and —for the historian—most challenging of all the phases of human events encountered in the record of this period. By this I mean the terrible, prolonged, and wasteful struggle that we know as World War I—and all that went with it.

I would like first to say a word about the total result of these two world wars in Europe. These wars were fought at the price of some tens of millions of lives, of untold physical destruction, of the destruction of the balance of forces on the Continent—at the price of rendering western Europe dangerously, perhaps fatefully, vulnerable to Soviet power. Both wars were fought, really, with a view to changing Germany: to correcting her behavior, to making the Germans something different from what

they were. Yet, today, if one were offered the chance of having back again the Germany of 1913—a Germany run by conservative but relatively moderate people, no Nazis and no Communists, a vigorous Germany, united and unoccupied, full of energy and confidence, able to play a part again in the balancing-off of Russian power in Europe—well, there would be objections to it from many quarters, and it wouldn't make everybody happy; but in many ways it wouldn't sound so bad, in comparison with our problems of today. Now, think what this means. When you tally up the total score of the two wars, in terms of their ostensible objective, you find that if there has been any gain at all, it is pretty hard to discern.

Does this not mean that something is terribly wrong here? Can it really be that all this bloodshed and sacrifice was just the price of sheer survival for the Western democracies in the twentieth

century? If we were to accept that conclusion, things would look pretty black;
for we would have to ask ourselves:
Where does all this end? If this was the
price of survival in the first half of the
twentieth century, what is survival going
to cost us in the second half? But plainly
this immense output of effort and sacrifice should have brought us something
more than just survival. And then, we
can only assume, some great miscalcula-
tions must have been made somewhere?
But where? Were they ours? Were they
our Allies'?

Eclipsed for many of us by the fresher
and more vivid recollections of World
War II, this first World War has become
in many respects the forgotten factor.
Yet all the lines of inquiry, it seems to
me, lead back to it. World War II
seemed really so extensively predeter-
mined; it developed and rolled its course
with the relentless logic of the last act
of a classical tragedy. And the main elements of that tragic situation—the sick-
ness and impatience of Germany, the
weakness of eastern Europe, the phenomenon of bolshevism in Russia, and
the weariness and debility in France and
England—all these things took their origin so clearly in the period of 1914–
20 that it seems to be here, if anywhere, that the real answers should be
sought.

I do not mean to say that there were
not still important things that could
have been done in the twenties and the
thirties, or perhaps even in the forties,
to avert the worst dangers and to press
the stream of events into more hopeful
channels. Thirty years is a long time in
the course of human events. The life of
an international community can always
be inclined to some extent, like a tree,
by persistent pressure in a single direction over a long space of time.

But I would submit that a significant
narrowing of the choices of the generations from 1920 to 1950 began with the
outbreak of violence in 1914; that with
the subsequent emergence of a military
deadlock and the disappearance of hopes
for a compromise peace this process was
greatly advanced and that by the time
the fire of war had finally burned itself
out, and the Treaty of Versailles had
been signed, the area in which Western
statesmen, and above all American
statesmen, could act to restore genuine
health and peace to Western civilization, and to give that civilization
strength to withstand the growing challenge from the East, had been grievously and tragically narrowed.

So we come back to the fact that much
of the cause for the decline in our security in the West lay with the course
and outcome of the first World War.
And for this reason our own part in it deserves the most careful scrutiny. . . .

In the first place, with respect to the
origins of the war: let us note that there
was for long no understanding in this
country that either the origins or the
issues of the war were of any concern to
us. Speaking in 1916, President Wilson
said that with the objects and causes of
the war "we are not concerned. The ob-
scure foundations from which its stu-
pendous flood has burst forth we are not
interested to search for or explore." [1]
"America," he said on a later occasion,
"did not at first see the full meaning of
the war. It looked like a natural raking
out of the pent-up jealousies and rivalries of the complicated politics of Europe." [2] Here, we may note, there was
no recognition that what might be at

[1] Address to the First Annual Assemblage of
the League to Enforce Peace, May 27, 1916.
[2] Speech on the "S.S. George Washington,"
July 4, 1919.

issue in the European war was anything that concerned us. There was the same denial we saw in the case of the Far East—of the legitimacy of the real interests and aspirations of other peoples, the same dismissal of these things as unsubstantial and unworthy of our attention, as "jealousies and rivalries" too silly, too "complicated," to deserve our respect.

Proceeding on this basis, it was logical that the only American interest in the war we were inclined to recognize for a long time was the defense of our neutral rights according to the established laws of maritime warfare, as they had been known in the past. We did not understand that new modalities of warfare and new weapons—above all, the total blockade and the submarine—had rendered obsolete some of the more important of these rules. Not only had their observance become physically impracticable, but each side had come to feel that its chances of victory and survival depended on the violation of one or another of them. Either side would have preferred to accept war with us rather than refrain from violating certain ones of them. This meant that a strict insistence by us on their observance could eventually lead us, theoretically, into war with both belligerents— a paradoxical ending for a policy designed to keep us out of war.

Looking backward today on these endless disputes between our government and the belligerents over neutral rights, it seems hard to understand how we could have attached so much importance to them. They irritated both belligerents and burdened our relations with them, and I find it hard to believe that they involved our national honor. It might be our privilege to defend the rights of our citizens to travel on belligerent vessels, but it was hardly a duty, unless we chose to define it as a duty to ourselves.

As time went on, there grew up, of course, alongside this outlook, something quite different: a realization of the danger of defeat that confronted the Entente powers and an awareness of the damage that would be done to our world position by the elimination of England as a strong force in the world. In addition to this, the superiority of British propaganda, and other factors, began to work to the benefit of the Allied cause. The result was a gradual growth of pro-Allied sentiment, and particularly in the minds of the responsible American leaders. This sentiment was enough to cause Wilson and House to water down our neutrality policy for the benefit of the British and to make cautious efforts to stop the war, in 1915 and 1916, as the best means of averting the danger of a British defeat. But this pro-Ally feeling was never sufficient to constitute, for the national consciousness as a whole, adequate justification for entering the war; and you will remember that our entry, when it came, was over an issue of neutrality.

Once in the war, we had no difficulty in discovering—and lost no time in doing so—that the issues involved in it were of the greatest significance to us.

It is surely a curious characteristic of democracy: this amazing ability to shift gears overnight in one's ideological attitudes, depending on whether one considers one's self at war or at peace. Day before yesterday, let us say, the issues at stake between ourselves and another power were not worth the life of a single American boy. Today, nothing else counts at all; our cause is holy; the cost is no consideration; violence must know no limitations short of unconditional surrender.

Now I know the answer to this one. A democracy is peace-loving. It does not like to go to war. It is slow to rise to provocation. When it has once been provoked to the point where it must grasp the sword, it does not easily forgive its adversary for having produced this situation. The fact of the provocation then becomes itself the issue. Democracy fights in anger—it fights for the very reason that it was forced to go to war. It fights to punish the power that was rash enough and hostile enough to provoke it—to teach that power a lesson it will not forget, to prevent the thing from happening again. Such a war must be carried to the bitter end.

This is true enough, and if nations could afford to operate in the moral climate of individual ethics, it would be understandable and acceptable. But I sometimes wonder whether in this respect a democracy is not uncomfortably similar to one of those prehistoric monsters with a body as long as this room and a brain the size of a pin: he lies there in his comfortable primeval mud and pays little attention to his environment; he is slow to wrath—in fact, you practically have to whack his tail off to make him aware that his interests are being disturbed; but, once he grasps this, he lays about him with such blind determination that he not only destroys his adversary but largely wrecks his native habitat. You wonder whether it would not have been wiser for him to have taken a little more interest in what was going on at an earlier date and to have seen whether he could not have prevented some of these situations from arising instead of proceeding from an undiscriminating indifference to a holy wrath equally undiscriminating.

In any case, once we were at war, it did not appear to us that our greatest danger might still lie precisely in too long a continuation of the war, in the destruction of Europe's equilibrium, and in the sapping of the vital energies of the European peoples. It did not appear to us then that the greatest interest we had in the war was still that it should be brought to an end as soon as possible on a basis involving a minimum maladjustment and as much stability as possible for the future. Prior to our entry into the war, many people had thought that way. As late as January, 1917, Wilson was still arguing against total victory. A "peace forced upon the loser, a victor's terms imposed upon the vanquished," he said, "would be accepted in humiliation, under duress, at an intolerable sacrifice, and would leave a sting, a resentment, a bitter memory upon which terms of peace would rest . . . as upon quicksand."[3] But, once we were in the war, these ideas were swept away by the powerful currents of war psychology. We were then as strong as anybody else in our determination that the war should be fought to the finish of a total victory.

Considerations of the power balance argued against total victory. Perhaps it was for this very reason that people in this country rejected them so emphatically and sought more sweeping and grandiose objectives, for the accomplishment of which total victory could plausibly be represented as absolutely essential.[4] In any case, a line of thought grew up, under Wilson's leadership, which provided both rationale and objective for our part in fighting the war to a bitter end. Germany was militaristic

[3] Address to the Senate, January 22, 1917.
[4] This was not true of Wilson—at least in the beginning of 1917. His mind was able to entertain simultaneously thoughts of peace without victory and expansive concepts of a future world order which explicitly rejected the balance of power.

and antidemocratic. The Allies were fighting to make the world safe for democracy. Prussian militarism had to be destroyed to make way for the sort of peace we wanted. This peace would not be based on the old balance of power. Who, as Wilson said, could guarantee equilibrium under such a system? It would be based this time on a "community of power," on "an organized common peace," on a League of Nations which would mobilize the conscience and power of mankind against aggression. Autocratic government would be done away with. Peoples would themselves choose the sovereignty under which they wished to reside. Poland would achieve her independence, as would likewise the restless peoples of the Austro-Hungarian Empire. There would be open diplomacy this time; peoples, not governments, would run things. Armaments would be reduced by mutual agreement. The peace would be just and secure.

In the name of such principles you could fight a war to the end. A future so brilliant would surely wash away the follies and brutalities of the war, redress its injuries, heal the wounds it had left. This theory gave us justification both for continuing the war to its bitter and terrible end—to the end described by that young German soldier in the military hospital—and at the same time for refusing to preoccupy ourselves with the practical problems and maladjustments to which the course of hostilities was leading. Under the protecting shadow of this theory, the guns continued their terrible work for a final year and a half after our entry. Under the shadow of this theory Wilson went to Versailles unprepared to face the sordid but all-important details of the day of reckoning. Under this theory he suffered his tragic and historic failure. Under this theory things advanced with a deadly logic and precision to a peace which was indeed "forced upon the loser, a victor's terms imposed upon the vanquished, accepted in humiliation, under duress"—a peace that did indeed leave a sting, a resentment, a bitter memory, and upon which its own terms came later to rest "as upon quicksand."

And the tragedy of this outcome was not substantially mitigated by the fact that we were not signatories to the Treaty of Versailles and kept ourselves aloof from its punitive provisions. The damage had been done. The equilibrium of Europe had been shattered. Austria-Hungary was gone. There was nothing effective to take its place. Germany, smarting from the sting of defeat and plunged into profound social unrest by the breakup of her traditional institutions, was left nevertheless as the only great united state in central Europe. Russia was no longer there, as a possible reliable ally, to help France contain German power. From the Russian plain there leered a single hostile eye, skeptical of Europe's values, rejoicing at all Europe's misfortunes, ready to collaborate solely for the final destruction of her spirit and her pride. Between Russia and Germany were only the pathetic new states of eastern and central Europe, lacking in domestic stability and the traditions of statesmanship—their peoples bewildered, uncertain, vacillating between brashness and timidity in the exercise of the unaccustomed responsibilities of independence. And to the other side of Germany were France and England, reeling, themselves, from the vicissitudes of the war, wounded far more deeply than they themselves realized, the plume of their manhood gone, their world positions shaken.

Truly, this was a peace which had the tragedies of the future written into it as by the devil's own hand. It was a peace, as the French historian Bainville said, which was too mild for the hardships it contained. And this was the sort of peace you got when you allowed war hysteria and impractical idealism to lie down together in your mind, like the lion and the lamb; when you indulged yourself in the colossal conceit of thinking that you could suddenly make international life over into what you believed to be your own image; when you dismissed the past with contempt, rejected the relevance of the past to the future, and refused to occupy yourself with the real problems that a study of the past would suggest.

But suppose you hadn't taken this line. Would things have been different? Was there another line you could take?

It does seem to me there was.

You might have begun, I should think, with a recognition of the importance to us of what was brewing in Europe in those years before the outbreak of war. You will remember that Wilson dismissed all this as something we were not even interested to examine.

Yet, was it all so silly, so unworthy of attention? I said in the beginning that some of the causes of the war were deep ones. The absence of a major war on the Continent during the century before 1914 had rested on a balance of power which presupposed the existence of France, Germany, Austria-Hungary, and Russia as dominant elements—and all of this flanked by an England instinctively conscious of her stake in the preservation of the balance among them and prepared to hover vigilantly about the fringes of the Continent, tending its equilibrium as one might tend a garden, yet always with due regard for the preservation of her own maritime supremacy and the protection of her overseas empire. In this complicated structure lay concealed not only the peace of Europe but also the security of the United States. Whatever affected it was bound to affect us. And all through the latter part of the nineteenth century things were happening which *were* bound to affect it: primarily the gradual shift of power from Austria-Hungary to Germany. This was particularly important because Austria-Hungary had not had much chance of becoming a naval and commercial rival to England, whereas Germany definitely did have such a chance and was foolish enough to exploit it aggressively, with a chip on her shoulder, in a way that gave the British a deep sense of concern and insecurity.

It is not only in retrospect that these things are visible.

In the winter of 1913 there appeared, anonymously, and in an English magazine (because no American magazine would take it), an article written by an American diplomatist of the time, Mr. Lewis Einstein.[5] In this article, Mr. Einstein drew attention to the storm clouds gathering over Europe, to the depth of the Anglo-German antagonism, to the danger that war might arise from some relatively insignificant incident, and to the effect that such a war might have on the equilibrium and stability of Europe. He then went on to trace out the significance of such a European war for the security of the United States. He never doubted that we would have to intervene to save England, if the alternative were clearly her destruction. But he warned against the assumption that we would not be affected by any drastic

[5] *National Review,* LX (January, 1913), 736–750.

alteration either way in the balance of forces in Europe:

Unperceived by many Americans, the European balance of power is a political necessity which can alone sanction on the Western Hemisphere the continuance of an economic development unhandicapped by the burden of extensive armaments.
. . . The disappearance or diminution of any one state in Europe would be a calamity, varying with its degree. . . .
It is no affair of the United States even though England were defeated, so long as the general balance is preserved. But if ever decisive results are about to be registered of a nature calculated to upset what has for centuries been the recognized political fabric of Europe, America can remain indifferent thereto only at its own eventual cost. If it then neglects to observe that the interests of the nations crushed are likewise its own, America will be guilty of political blindness which it will later rue.

Now you could, it seems to me, have taken this view—so well substantiated by the subsequent course of events—as your point of departure, let us say, from 1913. You might then, departing from the recognition that serious troubles *were* brewing in Europe and that our own interests *were* endangered, have seen to it that this country provided itself right then and there with something in the way of an armed establishment, so that our word would carry some weight and be listened to in the councils of the powers. When war broke out, you could have ignored the nonsensical timidities of technical neutrality and used our influence to achieve the earliest possible termination of a war that nobody could really win. Admittedly, if there were any possibility of this, it was in the first months of the war, and we would have had to be armed. If this had not succeeded, then you would have had to car-

ry on through the war, exercising what moderating influence you could, avoiding friction with the belligerents on minor matters, holding your power in reserve for the things that counted. And if you finally had to intervene to save the British from final defeat (which I am quite prepared to accept as a valid ground for intervention), then you could have gone in frankly for the avowed purpose both of doing this and of ending the war as rapidly as possible; you could have refrained from moralistic slogans, refrained from picturing your effort as a crusade, kept open your lines of negotiation to the enemy, declined to break up his empires and overthrow his political system, avoided commitments to the extremist war aims of your allies, retained your freedom of action, exploited your bargaining power flexibly with a view to bringing its full weight to bear at the crucial moments in order to achieve the termination of hostilities with a minimum prejudice to the future stability of the Continent.

All these things, as I say, you might conceivably have done. If you ask me, "Can you guarantee that this would have produced a better outcome and a happier future?" my answer is, "Of course not." I can say only that I fail to see how it could have produced a much worse one. And I can say that it would have been a conceptual framework more closely related to the realities of the world we live in and that in the long run—in the law of averages—conduct realistically motivated is likely to be more effective than conduct unrealistically motivated.

But I think I hear one great, and even indignant, objection to what I have suggested; and I must speak to it before I close. People will say to me: You know that what you have suggested was totally impossible from the standpoint of public opinion; that people in general had no idea that our interests were affected by what was going on in Europe in 1913; that they would never have dreamed of spending real money for armaments in time of peace; that they would never have gone into a war deliberately, as a result of cold calculation about the balance of power elsewhere; that they would have made war only upon direct provocation; that they could never have been brought to forgive such provocation and to refrain from pressing such a war to its final conclusion. And you know that they would not have been happy unless they had been able to clothe their military effort in the language of idealism and to persuade themselves that anything so important as Americans fighting on foreign soil had to end with a basic alteration of the terms of life among nations and a settlement of this business for once and for all. You—these people will say to me—hold yourself out as a realist, and yet none of these things you are talking about were ever even within the realm of practical possibility from the standpoint of domestic realities in our own country.

I have no quarrel with this argument. I am even going to concede it. I do think that political leaders might have made greater efforts than they did, from time to time, to inform themselves and to tell people the true facts, and I think people might even have understood them and been grateful to them if they had. But let that go and say that basically the argument is sound. I still have one thing to say about it.

I am not talking here about the behavior of Woodrow Wilson or Colonel House or Robert Lansing. I am talking about the behavior of the United States

of America. History does not forgive us our national mistakes because they are explicable in terms of our domestic politics. If you say that mistakes of the past were unavoidable because of our domestic predilections and habits of thought, you are saying that what stopped us from being more effective than we were was democracy, as practiced in this country. And, if that is true, let us recognize it and measure the full seriousness of it—and find something to do about it. A nation which excuses its own failures by the sacred untouchableness of its own habits can excuse itself into complete disaster. I said in the first of these lectures that the margin in which it is given to us to commit blunders has been drastically narrowed in the last fifty years. If it was the workings of our democracy that were inadequate in the past, let us say so. Whoever thinks the future is going to be easier than the past is certainly mad. And the system under which we are going to have to continue to conduct foreign policy is, I hope and pray, the system of democracy.

DIPLOMACY IN THE MODERN WORLD

. . . I see the most serious fault of our past policy formulation to lie in something that I might call the legalistic-moralistic approach to international problems. This approach runs like a red skein through our foreign policy of the last fifty years. It has in it something of the old emphasis on arbitration treaties, something of the Hague Conferences and schemes for universal disarmament, something of the more ambitious American concepts of the role of international law, something of the League of Nations and the United Nations, something of the Kellogg Pact, something of the idea of a universal "Article 51" past, something of the belief in World Law and

World Government. But it is none of these, entirely. Let me try to describe it.

It is the belief that it should be possible to suppress the chaotic and dangerous aspirations of governments in the international field by the acceptance of some system of legal rules and restraints. This belief undoubtedly represents in part an attempt to transpose the Anglo-Saxon concept of individual law into the international field and to make it applicable to governments as it is applicable here at home to individuals. It must also stem in part from the memory of the origin of our own political system—from the recollection that we were able, through acceptance of a common institutional and juridical framework, to reduce to harmless dimensions the conflicts of interest and aspiration among the original thirteen colonies and to bring them all into an ordered and peaceful relationship with one another. Remembering this, people are unable to understand that what might have been possible for the thirteen colonies in a given set of circumstances might not be possible in the wider international field.

It is the essence of this belief that, instead of taking the awkward conflicts of national interest and dealing with them on their merits with a view to finding the solutions least unsettling to the stability of international life, it would be better to find some formal criteria of a juridical nature by which the permissible behavior of states could be defined. There would then be judicial entities competent to measure the actions of governments against these criteria and to decide when their behavior was acceptable and when unacceptable. Behind all this, of course, lies the American assumption that the things for which other peoples in this world are apt to contend are for the most part neither creditable nor important and might justly be expected to take second place behind the desirability of an orderly world, untroubled by international violence. To the American mind, it is implausible that people should have positive aspirations, and ones that they regard as legitimate, more important to them than the peacefulness and orderliness of international life. From this standpoint, it is not apparent why other peoples should not join us in accepting the rules of the game in international politics, just as we accept such rules in the competition of sport in order that the game may not become too cruel and too destructive and may not assume an importance we did not mean it to have.

If they were to do this, the reasoning runs, then the troublesome and chaotic manifestations of the national ego could be contained and rendered either unsubstantial or subject to easy disposal by some method familiar and comprehensible to our American usage. Departing from this background, the mind of American statesmanship, stemming as it does in so large a part from the legal profession in our country, gropes with unfailing persistence for some institutional framework which would be capable of fulfilling this function.

I cannot undertake in this short lecture to deal exhaustively with this thesis or to point out all the elements of unsoundness which I feel it contains. But some of its more outstanding weaknesses are worthy of mention.

In the first place, the idea of the subordination of a large number of states to an international juridical regime, limiting their possibilities for aggression and injury to other states, implies that these are all states like our own, reasonably content with their international borders and status, at least to the extent that they would be willing to refrain from pressing for change without international agreement. Actually, this has generally been true only of a portion of international society. We tend to underestimate the violence of national maladjustments and discontents elsewhere in the world if we think that they would always appear to other people as less important than the preservation of the juridical tidiness of international life.

Second, while this concept is often associated with a revolt against nationalism, it is a curious thing that it actually tends to confer upon the concept of nationality and national sovereignty an absolute value it did not have before. The very principle of "one government, one vote," regardless of physical or political differences between states, glorifies the concept of national sovereignty and makes it the exclusive form of participation in international life. It envisages a world composed exclusively of sovereign national states with a full equality of status. In doing this, it ignores the tremendous variations in the firmness and soundness of national divisions: the fact that the origins of state borders and national personalities were in many instances fortuitous or at least poorly related to realities. It also ignores the law of change. The national state pattern is not, should not be, and cannot be a fixed and static thing. By nature, it is an unstable phenomenon in a constant state of change and flux. History has shown that the will and the capacity of individual peoples to contribute to their world environment is constantly changing. It is only logical that the organizational forms (and what else are such things as borders and governments?) should change with them. The function of a system of international relationships is not to inhibit this process

of change by imposing a legal strait jacket upon it but rather to facilitate it: to ease its transitions, to temper the asperities to which it often leads, to isolate and moderate the conflicts to which it gives rise, and to see that these conflicts do not assume forms too unsettling for international life in general. But this is a task for diplomacy, in the most old-fashioned sense of the term. For this, law is too abstract, too inflexible, too hard to adjust to the demands of the unpredictable and the unexpected.

By the same token, the American concept of world law ignores those means of international offense—those means of the projection of power and coercion over other peoples—which by-pass institutional forms entirely or even exploit them against themselves: such things as ideological attack, intimidation, penetration, and disguised seizure of the institutional paraphernalia of national sovereignty. It ignores, in other words, the device of the puppet state and the set of techniques by which states can be converted into puppets with no formal violation of, or challenge to, the outward attributes of their sovereignty and their independence.

This is one of the things that have caused the peoples of the satellite countries of eastern Europe to look with a certain tinge of bitterness on the United Nations. The organization failed so completely to save them from domination by a great neighboring country, a domination no less invidious by virtue of the fact that it came into being by processes we could not call "aggression." And there is indeed some justification for their feeling, because the legalistic approach to international affairs ignores in general the international significance of political problems and the deeper sources of international instability. It assumes that civil wars will remain civil and not grow into international wars. It assumes the ability of each people to solve its own internal political problems in a manner not provocative of its international environment. It assumes that each nation will always be able to construct a government qualified to speak for it and cast its vote in the international arena and that this government will be acceptable to the rest of the international community in this capacity. It assumes, in other words, that domestic issues will not become international issues and that the world community will not be put in the position of having to make choices between rival claimants for power within the confines of the individual state.

Finally, this legalistic approach to international relations is faulty in its assumptions concerning the possibility of sanctions against offenses and violations. In general, it looks to collective action to provide such sanction against the bad behavior of states. In doing so, it forgets the limitations on the effectiveness of military coalition. It forgets that, as a circle of military associates widens in any conceivable political-military venture, the theoretical total of available military strength may increase, but only at the cost of compactness and ease of control. And the wider a coalition becomes, the more difficult it becomes to retain political unity and general agreement on the purposes and effects of what is being done. As we are seeing in the case of Korea, joint military operations against an aggressor have a different meaning for each participant and raise specific political issues for each one which are extraneous to the action in question and affect many other facets of international life. The wider the circle of military associates, the more cumbersome the problem of political control

over their actions, and the more circumscribed the least common denominator of agreement. This law of diminishing returns lies so heavily on the possibilities for multilateral military action that it makes it doubtful whether the participation of smaller states can really add very much to the ability of the great powers to assure stability of international life. And this is tremendously important, for it brings us back to the realization that even under a system of world law the sanction against destructive international behavior might continue to rest basically, as it has in the past, on the alliances and relationships among the great powers themselves. There might be a state, or perhaps more than one state, which all the rest of the world community together could not successfully coerce into following a line of action to which it was violently averse. And if this is true, where are we? It seems to me that we are right back in the realm of the forgotten art of diplomacy from which we have spent fifty years trying to escape.

These, then, are some of the theoretical deficiencies that appear to me to be inherent in the legalistic approach to international affairs. But there is a greater deficiency still that I should like to mention before I close. That is the inevitable association of legalistic ideas with moralistic ones: the carrying-over into the affairs of states of the concepts of right and wrong, the assumption that state behavior is a fit subject for moral judgment. Whoever says there is a law must of course be indignant against the lawbreaker and feel a moral superiority to him. And when such indignation spills over into military contest, it knows no bounds short of the reduction of the lawbreaker to the point of complete submissiveness—namely, unconditional surrender. It is a curious thing, but it is true, that the legalistic approach to world affairs, rooted as it unquestionably is in a desire to do away with war and violence, makes violence more enduring, more terrible, and more destructive to political stability than did the older motives of national interest. A war fought in the name of high moral principle finds no early end short of some form of total domination.

In this way, we see that the legalistic approach to international problems is closely identified with the concept of total war and total victory, and the manifestations of the one spill over only too easily into the manifestations of the other. And the concept of total war is something we would all do well to think about a little in these troubled times. This is a relatively new concept, in Western civilization at any rate. It did not really appear on the scene until World War I. It characterized both of these great world wars, and both of them—as I have pointed out—were followed by great instability and disillusionment. But it is not only a question now of the desirability of this concept; it is a question of its feasibility. Actually, I wonder whether even in the past total victory was not really an illusion from the standpoint of the victors. In a sense, there is no total victory short of genocide, unless it be a victory over the minds of men. But the total military victories are rarely victories over the minds of men. And we now face the fact that it is very questionable whether in a new global conflict there could ever be any such thing as total *military* victory. I personally do not believe that there could. There might be a great weakening of the armed forces of one side or another, but I think it out of the question that there should be such a thing as

a general and formal submission of the national will on either side. The attempt to achieve this unattainable goal, however, could wreak upon civilization another set of injuries fully as serious as those caused by World War I or World War II, and I leave it to you to answer the question as to how civilization could survive them.

It was asserted not long ago by a prominent American that "war's very object is victory" and that "in war there can be no substitute for victory." Perhaps the confusion here lies in what is meant by the term "victory." Perhaps the term is actually misplaced. Perhaps there can be such a thing as "victory" in a battle, whereas in war there can be only the achievement or nonachievement of your objectives. In the old days, wartime objectives were generally limited and practical ones, and it was common to measure the success of your military operations by the extent to which they brought you closer to your objectives. But where your objectives are moral and ideological ones and run to changing the attitudes and traditions of an entire people or the personality of a regime, then victory is probably something not to be achieved entirely by military means or indeed in any short space of time at all; and perhaps that is the source of our confusion.

In any case, I am frank to say that I think there is no more dangerous delusion, none that has done us a greater disservice in the past or that threatens to do us a greater disservice in the future, than the concept of total victory. And I fear that it springs in large measure from the basic faults in the approach to international affairs which I have been discussing here. If we are to get away from it, this will not mean that we shall have to abandon our respect for international law, or our hopes for its future usefulness as the gentle civilizer of events which I mentioned in one of the earlier lectures. Nor will it mean that we have to go in for anything that can properly be termed "appeasement" —if one may use a word so cheapened and deflated by the abuse to which it has been recently subjected. But it will mean the emergence of a new attitude among us toward many things outside our borders that are irritating and unpleasant today—an attitude more like that of the doctor toward those physical phenomena in the human body that are neither pleasing nor fortunate—an attitude of detachment and soberness and readiness to reserve judgment. It will mean that we will have the modesty to admit that our own national interest is all that we are really capable of knowing and understanding—and the courage to recognize that if our own purposes and undertakings here at home are decent ones, unsullied by arrogance or hostility toward other people or delusions of superiority, then the pursuit of our national interest can never fail to be conducive to a better world. This concept is less ambitious and less inviting in its immediate prospects than those to which we have so often inclined, and less pleasing to our image of ourselves. To many it may seem to smack of cynicism and reaction. I cannot share these doubts. Whatever is realistic in concept, and founded in an endeavor to see both ourselves and others as we really are, cannot be illiberal.

Frank Tannenbaum:

THE AMERICAN TRADITION IN FOREIGN POLICY

Frank Tannenbaum is Professor of Latin-American History at Columbia University and has done most of his writing about Latin America and labor. Always provocative and independent in his ideas, however, his interests have ranged beyond any narrow specialization. The almost simultaneous publication of Kennan's book and of a still more vigorous plea for "realism" in foreign policy by Hans J. Morgenthau, Professor of Political Science at the University of Chicago, led Tannenbaum to make a spirited rejoinder to these contemporary critics of idealism as represented in Wilson's peace program.

A GREAT debate on the character and purpose of American foreign policy has been precipitated by those who would persuade our people to abandon their humanitarian and pacific traditions and frankly adopt the doctrine of power politics and of the balance of power as the basis of their foreign pol-

Reprinted by permission from Frank Tannenbaum, "The Balance of Power Versus the Coördinate State," *Political Science Quarterly*, 67 (1952), 173–179, 189–197 and *The American Tradition in Foreign Policy* (Norman: University of Oklahoma Press, 1955), pp. 114–116, 117–119, and 123–124.

icy. This doctrine is confessedly, nay gleefully, amoral. It prides itself upon being realistic and takes Machiavelli as its great teacher. It is contemptuous of the simple beliefs of honest men, jeers at the sentimentalism of those who believe that men may strive for peace among nations, and looks upon democracy as a hindrance to skilled diplomacy. It looks with a certain derisive superiority upon the great leaders of this nation from Jefferson and John Quincy Adams to Woodrow Wilson and Franklin Delano Roosevelt and describes them as moralistic and sentimental, and suggests that our models ought to be Richelieu, Clemenceau and Bismarck. Its adherents believe that international wars instead of being made by men and supported by institutions humanly contrived have their origin in the nature of man himself and are inevitable. The best they foresee is an armed balance of power—until the next war—and after that, more skilled diplomacy toward the achievement of the same inevitable end, a new balance of power ending in a new war.

This dreadful doctrine has now won wide acceptance by teachers and scholars in the field of international relations and has, in fact, become the leading theme in such circles in many of our largest universities. It has become the *science* of international relations—and who would quarrel with science especially when it comes packaged in good clear English and from high sources? But it is not science. It is, in fact, only poor logic based upon false premises, and its claim to be a science is only a bit of unholy conceit. For what we are dealing with is not a tentative hypothesis put forth by humble men as a possible clue for other students to analyze, criticize, modify and reject—or partially accept. No, we are offered a doctrine for

national behavior which runs counter to the very essence of the American tradition and are told to accept it in the name of the national interest because this science has discovered what that interest is.

This debate is of greater import to the future of the United States than the long running argument between the "interventionists" and the "isolationists." Both of these accepted the basic American belief in international good will, in the doctrine of friendship among nations, in the right of the little nation to abide in security and without fear, in the possibility of finding a way to peace among nations, in the sanctity of international treaties, in the authority of international law, and in the hope that the democratic way, by enhancing human dignity and widening human freedom, would ease the burden and conflict among men and nations. The "interventionists" and "isolationists" differed about how best to translate these ideas into formal policy, but they did not, with strikingly few exceptions, repudiate the doctrine by which this nation has lived from its very inception.

Now the advocates of *Realpolitik* would sweep away all of our old beliefs as foolish, sentimental and moralistic. They would have us build our future upon the concept of the balance of power in international relations, throw all morality and law out of the window as a hindrance and nuisance to skilled diplomacy, divide the world between Russia and ourselves, repudiating our past beliefs, as well as our promises, obligations and treaties that bind us to our many allies, and girdle ourselves by a permanent and huge military establishment—for what?—to carry the happy game of skilled diplomacy from one war to the next. Most of this is explicitly stated in the argument. Some of it, though not stated, is implicit, and constitutes a challenge to the democratic process itself. These doctrines, if adopted and implemented, would convert the United States into a centralized military empire, and in due time destroy the basic democratic institutions by which this government has prospered these many years.

This debate is just beginning. A good deal more will be heard of it in the coming years. The fact that so erudite a scholar as Professor Hans J. Morgenthau, of the University of Chicago, and so subtle a mind as George F. Kennan are the chief proponents of this dreadful doctrine in the United States will add zest to the debate. The appointment of Mr. Kennan as Ambassador to Russia gives his views immediate significance in American foreign policy. But the American people will not take this advice, for they cannot act upon it without ceasing to be both a Christian and a democratic people.

This essay is an attempt to state what has always been the American philosophy of international relations. It brings to the surface the beliefs and the ideals upon which this nation was built as a great federal system, and shows how these same commitments have shaped our foreign policy from the beginning.

We want to be clear on what the debate is about. One side believes that it is necessary, even inevitable, that the relations between nations be built upon the principle of the balance of power. The other believes that it is possible and desirable, if man wishes to save himself from destruction, to organize international relations on the basis of the coordinate state. The first derives its conclusions and its law from the modern national state system of Europe, the other from the experience of the federal

system of the United States, from the development of the Organization of American States, from the recent adoption of the principle of the coördinate state on which to frame the Commonwealth of Nations and from the federal history of Switzerland. These two different conceptions of the basis of international organization carry with them underlying assumptions of the nature of man, of the possible role of human institutions as well as implicit attitudes toward the democratic process. The international relations of the United States have unconsciously been dominated by the belief that the relations between states can be made to rest only upon the ideal mutuality, the equal right to abide in freedom and the dignity of all nations—great and small.

An international society, built upon the coördinate state, must of necessity behave differently from one resting upon the concept of centralized power. The first makes coöperation both the means and the ends of its policy. It can, in fact, have no other objectives. Its ends are determined by its means. Its objectives in international as in internal affairs can only be coöperation for the resolution of common difficulties, and its means can again only be coöperation. It accepts the doctrine of live and let live as a matter of course, for its own life is conceived of as a process of continuing accommodation within a world of nonviolent friction.

Friction and differences are taken for granted. They are recognized as a persistent phenomenon. There is no effort at an absolute or perfect solution. The meaning of peace is unwittingly redefined to mean, not the absence of serious difficulties or the disappearance of differences of interest, but the daily haggling over issues toward a workable compromise. An international society composed of "equal" members endowed with unequal resources requires the surrender of the "simplistic" notion of a "solution" of "problems." The very idea of "solution," and the concept of "problem" for which a permanent "solution" is to be had, are both felt to be delusive. There are no "problems" and no "solutions" in the complex of political society or in international relations. There are, in fact, no "social sciences" from which these final ends can be derived. And the beginning of wisdom in these matters is the recognition that man abides in a recalcitrant and imperfect universe.

The world is not fully malleable to the hand of man. All of life, all of society, all of international relations is a developing and changing series of forces upon which no stable form can be imposed by any method. The best that man may contrive are means toward a workable compromise so that change may take place without violence. Friction will go on, differences old and new will continually emerge, and no formula the "scientists," politicians and statesmen can devise will freeze the fleeting moment and permanently balk the hidden and contradictory flux that always moves through the world, and must do so as long as man survives on the face of the earth. These contradictory processes are life itself. If they ceased to be, life—personal, social or international—would also cease. The feasible is not a permanent "solution," but a channel for continuing adjustments among contradictory drives.

A substantial amount of balance between the forces of nature is essential to survival, but the balance is never absolute and is always changing. A stable world is best described as one of relative instability. It is in that sense that there are no solutions and no problems, either within the nation or between the nations. But these compromises can be made only between recognized and existing entities. These entities must not only exist, but be recognized as existing, whether they be men, institutions, societies, corporations or nations. The recognition of their existence implies an acknowledgment of a claim upon all other similar beings because they can only survive mutually, and cannot live in absolute isolation. The condition of mutuality is an equal opportunity to survival, which in turn requires the acceptance of the equal dignity of the existing entities mutually interdependent.

This is the meaning of the "coördinate state" in international relations. It implies a position of equal dignity. It has nothing to do with wealth, power, size, population or culture. It has everything to do with the recognition that compromise is a continuing means of nonviolent friction (peace). It has everything to do with the acknowledgment of the unique sense of "historic personality" which each state has of itself as the only basis of a friendly relationship. It is only if all the states continue to have equal dignity among themselves that changes in power and wealth can be absorbed without undue violence. That is the essence of federalism in international relations. The coördinate state relationship makes it possible to accept the inevitable growth of some and the decline of other states without war and without the loss of "face," because the changes are gradual and absorbed through a process of accommodation by all the members who are equal to each other. Federalism embodies these traits and has been illustrated in many ways by the history of the United States.

The essential character of the American system derives from a federal relationship of coördinate states. Our expectancies and demands upon the world are conditioned by that fact. This does not mean that we have not in our relations to the outside world committed grave errors, and on many occasions denied our own beliefs. The traditional twisting of the "British lion's tail" is but one example of a species of irresponsibility in international relations. Theodore Roosevelt's interference in the arbitration of the Alaska boundary dispute; his "I took the Panama Canal"; Wilson's intervention in Haiti and Santo Domingo; the Platt Amendment; the arbitrary senatorial action on Japanese migration; the century-long bullying of Mexico; the numerous landings of American marines in Central America; the indifference to the feelings of foreign nations often expressed in Congressional debates; our constant preachments and moralizations; the subordination of our foreign policies to domestic politics; the support of "big business" and American investors in foreign countries, sometimes without due regard to the legitimacy of their claims; the lack of sensitivity to foreign culture and foreign values and, since the Second World War, the conscious but faltering support of colonialism—these are all part of the story of our failure to abide by our own commitments.

However, these variations from our own professed ideas are the side currents at the edge of the broad stream of our foreign policy. The major drift of our relations with the rest of the world has with more or less consistency responded to the basic tradition of the coördinate state. We have, with the exception of the short but more than memorable episode of the Freedmen's Bureau and Reconstruction, never for long deviated from the idea of equal dignity of the state inside our own federal system, and have therefore never long permitted ourselves to act overtly toward other nations as if we were a centralized state, concerned primarily with the security that rests upon military force and military alliances. We have always sought our security either in isolation or in coöperation with other nations of equal dignity.

This conception of the equal dignity of the state is therefore fundamental to our own thinking about the world. Just what do we mean by the equal dignity of the state? This is a crucial question, for it defines the character of our own federal system. More than that, this concept of the equal dignity of the coöperating state not only represents a basis for our own federal system, but lies at the root of the Organization of American States. What is more, it is a similar concept, not uninfluenced by the American experience, which has come to govern the British Commonwealth of Nations. This same basic definition of the equal dignity of the related members has shaped the long-successful Swiss Confederation. We are therefore dealing with a general principle of organization, of which the American federal system is but a type. And this system of international organization stands in the world as a contrast to the alternative idea of the balance of power between states, and to the doctrines of power politics advanced by the schools of *Realpolitik*, of which Professor Hans Morgenthau and Mr. George Kennan are, at the moment, the most widely recognized proponents in the United States.*

* * *

* Frank Tannenbaum, "The Balance of Power Versus the Coördinate State," *Political Science Quarterly*, 67 (1952), 173–179. Reprinted by permission.

Wilson's Fourteen Points are part of the same story. They could only have been written by an American. The war could only have a moral purpose. It had to lead to a general association to guarantee the "political independence and territorial integrity" of great and small nations alike. Nothing else was worth the war. How clear this conviction was can be seen in Wilson's famous "peace without victory" speech, delivered before a joint session of Congress on January 22, 1917, three months before we entered the war.

This speech deserves the most careful consideration. The President of the United States was speaking for a nation at peace, striving to remain neutral, and giving utterance to the country's deepest convictions. He was, while arguing for peace, stating unconsciously the grounds upon which we would ultimately enter the war.

It must be a peace without victory. . . . Only a peace between equals can last. . . .
. . . The equality of nations upon which peace must be founded if it is to last must be an equality of rights. . . . Equality of territory or of resources there of course cannot be. . . . But no one asks or expects anything more than an equality of rights. . . .
. . . No peace can last, or ought to last, which does not recognize and accept the principle that . . . no right anywhere exists to hand peoples about from sovereignty to sovereignty as if they were property. . . .
. . . I am proposing, as it were, that the nations should with one accord adopt the doctrine of President Monroe as the doctrine of the world; that . . . every people should be left free to determine its own polity, its own way of development, unhindered, unthreatened, unafraid, the little along with the great and powerful.
. . . These are American principles,

American policies. We could stand for no others.[1]

For with us, security is only conceivable in a just world. That is where we differ from other peoples, and that is where the advocates of the doctrines of economic determinism and of power politics miss the point when they try to describe American motivation. To the American people, it is inconceivable that military security can rest upon injustice, upon power, upon the ill-gotten fruits of imperialism and oppression. Security must stem from the loyal coöperation of people associated in the common enterprise of peaceful existence in a recalcitrant universe. Power derived from conquest, exploitation, and abuse is insecure just because it is unjust, and is bound to fail when the crucial test arrives. The Fourteen Points of Wilson and the struggle in Paris for the making of the peace are illustrative of the issue at hand. The Fourteen Points were the American expression of faith in a world where decent men could live together in peace and dignity and where the small and great states would feel secure. . . .

The making of the peace, however, when the delegates gathered at Versailles nearly a year later, proved a different matter. Wilson's idealism and America's faith in a better world was there greatly compromised by the writing of terms which, in effect, largely repudiated both the purpose for which the United States had entered the war, and the Fourteen Points which Germany had accepted as a basis for ending it. When Wilson found himself faced with the realities of Europe, he compromised with the evil he had taken the American

[1] 64th Congress, 2nd Session, *Congressional Record*, Vol. LIV, Part 2 (January 22, 1917), 1741–43.

people into the war to destroy. He compromised in bitterness and in unhappiness. But he did it in the effort to rescue the League of Nations from the wreckage of America's hopes and ideals. For, in the League, at least, there was the promise that in the end the ideals of the American people would be fulfilled. The League would make a world where the little nations could be as safe as the big, and have their moral integrity and political equality secured.

The American people, however, defeated this effort because Wilson had destroyed their faith when he yielded to European diplomacy. Had Wilson stayed at home, or had he abandoned the conference and declared in the ringing words he was master of, that he would not bargain with evil, that the American people had not gone to war to rescue the imperial powers and guarantee them in their possessions, that he had not taken the people of the United States to war to destroy the German people but to save them and their conquerors as well from the dangers of future wars, he would not have lost his leadership, and he might have won both the League of Nations and an acceptable peace.

Colonel House emphasized this point. ". . . I do not believe that he utilized his commanding position. He was the *God on the mountain* [italics in the original] and his decisions regarding international matters were practically final. When he came to Europe and sat in with the prime ministers of the other states, he gradually lost his place as first citizen of the world." [2]

What in the end defeated Wilson, and the League of Nations as well, was not

just political chicanery, or personal hatreds, or Wilson's stubbornness, but also the bitter disillusionment of the American people when they discovered that they had been misled, not by their enemies, but by their allies. The bitterness turned against France, but especially against England. And the League of Nations was ultimately voted down in the United States Senate, not because it committed the United States to participate in world affairs, but because it sanctioned an unjust peace by tying up the League with the treaty. The League would seemingly confirm England, France, and Italy in their new gains. It would apparently increase the strangle hold of the imperial powers over subject peoples. It would saddle French militarism on Europe. It would make a mockery of the proposed self-determination of nations, which was so large a part of the American war ideal, just as the treaty negotiations had made a mockery of open covenants openly arrived at.

It is erroneous to assume, as is almost always done, that the defeat of the League of Nations was evidence of our disavowal of interest in world peace or in world affairs. The League of Nations, tied in as it was with the German Peace Treaty, was defeated because it seemed to confirm the militarism we had gone to war to eradicate. . . .

. . . What finally assured America's refusal to enter the international association it had brought into being was the conviction that the League of Nations and the peace denied, rather than affirmed, the ideals of freedom, justice, and the independence of the coördinate state in the international community.

Wilson's effort to salvage something out of the wreckage led both to a moral and political disaster. The disillusionment of the "lost generation" that fol-

[2] Charles Seymour, *American Diplomacy During the World War* (Baltimore, Johns Hopkins Press, 1934), 399.

lowed upon the heels of the futile crusade made America a lonely and isolated nation in more than the international sense.

We went into the war to "make the world safe for democracy"; we fought "a war against war"; we crossed the ocean a million strong to establish the principle of self-determination, and, when our allies confirmed what their worst enemies had said of them, we turned our backs upon them. We turned our backs upon them because they failed us. The League of Nations was but "a scrap of paper," and the real things were the secret treaties, the power positions, the economic arrangements, the indemnities, and the cynicism of an older diplomacy that we could not understand and would not bargain with. We did not abandon Europe. Europe abandoned us.

There is visible in this prolonged debate the "fundamental principle" the American people have pursued with a consistency that is as surprising as it is fascinating. For this ideal of the coordinate state has worked in the things we did as well as in those we failed to do. In the struggle over the League of Nations, as we have just seen, opponents argued that Europe was irremediable, set in its corrupt ways, and incapable of learning the American lesson of equality and anticolonialism, and that we ought therefore to stay out of Europe. The advocate of the League countered that Europe had been reformed, Americanized, so to speak, and would now, if we joined the League, adopt our principles of the coördinate state, and then turn towards a beneficent rather than oppressive foreign policy. The "isolationists" and the "joiners" were arguing their case on the same grounds, the first insisting that Europe could not, and the second, that it could be reformed—reformed meaning

learning to respect the political equality and territorial integrity of the independent nation.*

*   *   *

The Continental Congress, the United States, the Organization of American States, the League of Nations, the United Nations, the North Atlantic Pact, and the effort to stimulate a European union are all parts of the same story. In each of these instances, there is visible the common ideal of coöperation among equal states. How congenial that concept is to the American experience is illustrated at the very beginning of our history not only by the doctrine of equal legislative sovereignty for the colonies advanced by the early leaders as a proper basis for the organization of the British Empire, but in Benjamin Franklin's suggestion after the formation of the American Constitution that Europe follow our example and establish for itself a federal system. Benjamin Franklin was sagacious and experienced beyond most men and he not only knew the United States but had deep knowledge of England and the Continent. In the ripeness of his years, after helping frame the American Constitution, he felt that it represented a political system that Europe might well adopt for itself. In the year 1787, Franklin wrote to a European friend:

I send you enclosed the proposed new Federal Constitution for these States. I was engaged four months of the last summer in the Convention that formed it. . . . If it succeeds, I do not see why you might not in Europe carry the project of Good Henry the 4th into execution, by forming a Federal Union and One Grand Republic of all its different States and Kingdoms; by means

* From Frank Tannenbaum, *The American Tradition in Foreign Policy*. Copyright 1955, by the University of Oklahoma Press, Norman.

of a like Convention; for we had many interests to reconcile.[3]

The concept of federalism is, with the American people, bred in the bone as part of the idea of political freedom. We believe that security rests upon coöperation, that coöperation is possible only among equals, that equality eliminates the basic reason for political disruption because equals politically are "coördinate" in dignity and in rank, that this common identity is essential for different states to achieve that unity which makes them members of the same political family. International coöperation from our point of view requires that all participating members be insiders, and that such a fellowship is in the end an "indestructible union." That is why the concept of a "balance of power" is alien and repugnant to the American people. We have condemned in others the policies derived from that concept and have rejected them for ourselves. Illustrative of this attitude is President Wilson's statement: " . . . the center . . . of the old order was that unstable thing which we used to call 'balance of power' . . . a thing determined by the sword . . . thrown in on one side or the other."[4] And "If the future had nothing for us but a new attempt to keep the world at a right poise by a balance of power, the United States would take no interest, because she will join no combination of power that is not the combination of all of us."[5]

To the advocates of power politics and the balance of power, however, these American convictions and beliefs derived from their own experience are "intoxication with moral abstractions . . . which . . . has become the prevailing substitute for political thought."[6] And Wilson, because he advocated a League of Nations, was driven to "substituting for the concrete national interest of the United States the general postulate of a brave new world where the national interest of the United States, as that of all other nations, would disappear in a community of interest comprising mankind."[7] These same errors were committed by the leaders of the Second World War, Roosevelt and Hull. The reason for their failure is simple and obvious.

How could statesmen who boasted that they were not "believers in the idea of balance of power"—like a scientist not believing in the law of gravity—and who were out "to kill power politics," understand the very idea of the national interest which demanded, above all, protection from the power of others?[8]

The American mind, according to Dr. Hans Morgenthau, has been "weakened in its understanding of foreign policy by half a century of ever more complete intoxication with moral abstractions."[9] The difficulty with American foreign policy is that it is burdened with "utopianism, legalism, sentimentalism [and] . . . neo-isolationism."[10] It does not understand that

Foreign policy, like all politics, is in its essence a struggle for power, waged by sovereign nations for national advantage. . . . By its very nature this struggle is never

---

[3] Oct. 22, 1787 to Mr. Grand. *Documentary History of the Constitution of the United States of America,* Department of State, vol. IV (1905), pp. 341–342.
[4] Albert Shaw, *Messages and Papers of Woodrow Wilson* (New York, 1924), p. 584.
[5] *Ibid.,* p. 591.
[6] Hans J. Morgenthau, *In Defense of the National Interest* (New York, 1951), p. 4.
[7] *Ibid.,* p. 26.
[8] *Ibid.,* pp. 32–33.
[9] *Ibid.,* p. 39.
[10] *Ibid.,* p. 92.

ended, for the lust for power, and the fear of it, is never stilled. . . . In the life of nations peace is only respite from trouble— or the permanent peace of extinction.[11]

Our great mistake was to assume that the United Nations could be a substitute for the balance of power. We defined it in "utopian terms of permanent peace and non-competitive, trustful coöperation among the great powers." American policy is wrong because it is interested in the "well-being of all mankind." [12] A nation is under no obligation to keep a treaty. It is, in fact, an "iron law of international politics that legal obligations must yield to the national interest." There is apparently no difference between nations that "have a flair for throwing burdensome obligations overboard in an elegant, unobtrusive fashion, or of chiseling them away with the fine tools of legal misinterpretation" like France has done, and Russia and Germany who "have the disconcerting habit . . . of . . . announcing . . . that a treaty has become a 'scrap of paper'." These matters are, after all, only "the lawyers' concern" which the statesman can take in his stride in pursuit of the "national interest." Nor need the great powers be concerned about the interests of third parties; "great powers . . . have by tradition and logic . . . settled their disputes . . . over the regions where their interest, power and responsibilities were paramount." The business of statesmanship could not be carried on any other way.[13]

It is a legalistic illusion to believe that the United Nations is a substitute for power politics because it is obvious "from the political history of the human race that the balance of power and concomitant spheres of influence are of the very essence of international politics. They may be disregarded at the peril of those who choose to do so but they cannot be abolished." [14]

American policy, therefore, operates with "defective intellectual equipment." [15] Our difficulties derive from our failure to recognize that the "balance of power" is as much a law of politics as gravity is a law of physics and is illustrated by all of human history. This law which apparently is basic to the "science" of international relations has been understood by all the great statesmen, who, each in turn, have successfully ruined their nations and made a shambles out of all those parts of the world where they have been free to work out the "law" and practice the science. Now we too, who have prospered by refusing to apply the science or believe in its basic law, are urged, on grounds of the "national interest," to join the historical procession to national suicide by dividing the world between Russia and ourselves. The fact that it runs counter to every political instinct of the American people merely proves that we are possessed of a "defective intellectual equipment" and, if we consider it immoral and contrary to our experience to trade away the independence and freedom of other nations as part of the bargain, it shows that we are sentimental, moralistic, utopian and neo-isolationist and we can refuse to take this advice only at our own peril because the balance of power like the law of gravity will work its way regardless of what foolish men may do.

Now we submit that all this has nothing to do with science, and little to do

[11] *Ibid.*, p. 92.
[12] *Ibid.*, p. 114.
[13] *Ibid.*, pp. 142–146.

[14] *Ibid.*, pp. 154–155.
[15] *Ibid.*, p. 159.

with the infinitely complex influences that have shaped the history of man through time. We suspect that it is a very subjective and private view of the nature of man and of his role on earth. And that view seems to be that man is now and has always been in a sad estate from which he cannot extricate himself. He has no one to help him. He has no law to live by, no morality to support him; he has nothing except the "balance of power"—and if he will not believe in that, then God help him—but in this view of the world even that comfort is denied to man, for it could not abide any concept of a teleological universe. The interesting thing about this point of view is that it should either remain oblivious to or scorn the vast record of cooperative experience among men and nations, and that it should treat the relatively short and exceptional history of the European state system as equivalent to the history of the race across the face of time, and that it should deny the possibility and presumably the desirability of institutional development in the relations between nations. Institutions are presumably, by some undivulged "law," confined to grow only inside of the "sovereign" state. There must be no extra-national institutions; they would deny the "national interest" and make for "a brave new world" which is the greatest of political sins.

There is another statement of this theme of *Realpolitik* and the balance of power that comes from the influential and highly skilled pen of Mr. George F. Kennan.[16] In this exposition of the case, there is a kind of urbanity, a kind of sensitivity for the values and shortcomings of the American milieu and a kind of compassion for human frailty that

robs it of much of its sting. It is so gently, so persuasively stated, that the reader finds himself carried along almost to the point of agreement until he realizes that this modest and restrained presentation is, in fact, a repudiation of every value we hold:

I see the most serious fault of our past policy formulation to lie in something that I might call the legalistic-moralistic approach to international problems. This approach runs like a red skein through our foreign policy of the last fifty years. It has in it something of the old emphasis on arbitration treaties, something of the Hague Conferences and schemes for universal disarmament, something of the more ambitious American concepts of the role of international law, something of the League of Nations and the United Nations, something of the Kellogg Pact, something of the idea of a universal "Article 51" pact, something of the belief in World Law and World Government.[17]

This is more than a challenge to our international policies of the last fifty years. It is a denial of the American beliefs that have sustained American political life from the beginning; for our ideas of foreign policy are part and parcel of our belief in human freedom, in the equality of men, and in the dignity and independence of nations. The extenuating feature of Mr. Kennan's presentation is its lack of consistency. There is internal evidence that the author has not really made up his mind about these important matters. He is still ambivalent and groping for the truth, and the "balance of power" has not achieved the status of a "law" like the law of gravity. This is, in our view, a saving grace—but the damage has been done, for an influential voice has been added to the at-

[16] George F. Kennan, *American Diplomacy, 1900–1950* (Chicago, 1951).

[17] *Ibid.*, p. 95.

tempt to persuade the American people that their traditional policy based upon the coördinate state is wrong and has proved a failure.

The proof often presented by those who would force us off our beaten path is the failure of the League of Nations. A particular instance is made to serve the ends of a universal law. The League having failed, then all international organizations must fail. But the reasons for the failure were numerous. That the League was not based upon the idea of the coördinate state was, in our view, one of its major weaknesses. If all the members of that body had had an equal voice, Italy's attack upon Ethiopia would have been defeated, and sanctions both economic and military would have been effectively applied. It will be said in reply that the small powers would have committed the large ones to a possible war in which they would have borne a minor part. That may or may not be true. But the way to have avoided the greater tragedy which ultimately destroyed or weakened both the great and the small states was to have acted as the small states would have acted—to enforce the principle that in the modern world there are no separate interests for the small or the large state, that their destinies are collectively involved in each other, and that the violation, by war and oppression, of the independence of even the smallest power is, in the end, the denial of the possible survival without war even of the largest power. For such violation, whatever the grounds on which it is justified, is in effect the building of aggressive power against other nations until they, too, are placed in jeopardy. In this view of the matter, the structuring of international organization on the coördinate state is the alternative to the balance of power,

and to security without permanent militarization. Nor must we permit ourselves to be confused by the argument that the United Nations has failed and that the Atlantic Security Pact is the true substitute in the form of a military alliance. The Atlantic Security Pact is conceived of as a temporary and instrumental association of a defensive character organized for the purpose of implementing the ideal of the United Nations. It has nothing to do with the balance of power idea and less to do with dividing the world into spheres of interest between Russia and ourselves. Its objectives are aimed precisely at an attempt to prevent the permanent militarization which dividing the world into spheres of influence would require, and to escape the destruction of the democratic process which would follow in its wake.

The American people will not accept the program. They will not consent to the destruction of all that a hundred and fifty years of democratic life has brought them for the sake of being the masters of that part of the world which they could lay hold of. They will not do it because it runs against their grain, and because they have an alternative which seems more difficult to those hypnotized by the ideal of force and craft but is, in fact, easier and more consistent with our own traditional way with other people, and one we know how to live with because we have always done so. And that is the organization of as much of the world as we can upon the basis of the coördinate state, not for the sake of achieving a balance of power, but for the sake of building a basis of common defense upon a system of collective security open to all the nations of the world who wish to join it, without losing their independence or their dignity. It may prove impossible under present conditions to build such a system without having to fight a war with Russia, but then at least we will be fighting, as we did before, for the thing we consider worth defending with our lives and treasure. Equally important, our allies and partners will be fighting for things as dear to them as ours are to us. They will find their own values secured in a common defense and a common victory. And our enemy, Russia, will find the peoples of its own satellites striving to enter our common security system just because it is made to rest on the ideal of the coördinate state.

A balance of power settlement would lead our many allies and associates to conclude that they are mere pawns in a game of international politics played at their expense. They would cease to be partners in a great cause; for the division of the world into spheres of influence would automatically destroy the basis of the partnership in the West. That partnership rests upon the assumption that all the members are equal, that their rights cannot be bargained away, that they have to be consulted, that they have to consent freely to changes that affect them. It also rests upon the assumption that there are *no* spheres of influence—that the United States has no rights greater than the least of its members, and that the defensive is a joined defense of a common interest, but that the common interest rests upon the particular and unique political personality of each member. It assumes a coördinate relationship, not the position of a great power with many satellite powers. The mere acceptance of the idea of a balance of power would undermine the basis of the relationship among free partners formed together and would convert it into an empire with satellites to be ordered about. It would convert

the United States from a federal republic to an empire and ultimately destroy the republic. That is what the proposal really means, and that is why it will be resisted by the American people.

Such an arrangement would lead our friends to fall away from us feeling that they had been betrayed, as, in fact, they would have been. They, too, would seek the best bargain—temporarily—and play for higher stakes when the occasion offered. We would find ourselves weaker in the international field, not stronger. We would have voluntarily accepted a great moral defeat, and the power derived from a common cause among nations, all of whom felt identified through interest, belief and outlook, would have been irretrievably lost. The only remaining hope that an association of coördinate states could be gathered together to resist the attempt by Russia to dominate the world would evaporate. It is difficult to foresee a day more dark and hopeless than the one on which the American people could be persuaded to seek a temporary peace through deliberately sacrificing the principle of voluntary association among nations, and agree to divide the world between Russia and the United States.

No. With all of our shortcomings and failings, we will not accept the new science and follow the "will-o'-the-wisp" of *Realpolitik*. We will not abandon the faith we have lived by, nor deny the other nations the right to live in freedom and without fear. Our commitments are to a world of free men working together in free nations. The democratic faith that lies at the base of everything we cherish is the overriding law of American policy both at home and abroad. We cannot surrender our belief in the equal dignity of little nations without, in the end, abandoning our belief in the equal dignity of men. We will, if we have to, resist to the death the effort to subvert the world to a totalitarian despotism, but we will not bargain with it at the expense of other people and to the destruction of that sense of human integrity and national morality which is part of the substance of our very being. This may not be "science," but that is the way it is. We can do no other. Therein lies our strength.*

* Frank Tannenbaum, "The Balance of Power Versus the Coördinate State," *Political Science Quarterly*, 67 (1952), 189–197. Reprinted by permission.

Suggestions for Additional Reading

The literature on the Treaty of Versailles, on Wilson's role at Paris, and on the general question of what constitutes sound foreign policy is so extensive that only a few of the more directly useful items can be suggested here.

What errors Wilson did or did not commit at Paris can be better judged after reading some full-length account of the Peace Conference. Ray Stannard Baker's two volumes, *Woodrow Wilson and World Settlement* (New York, 1923), are colorfully written and sympathetic to Wilson. The selection here from Paul Birdsall's *Versailles Twenty Years After* (New York, 1941) can well be supplemented by further reading in this most effective defense of Wilson, while all the criticisms of Wilson's procedure are considered more fully in Thomas A. Bailey, *Woodrow Wilson and the Lost Peace* (New York, 1944).

Other American participants in the Peace Conference have been critical in varying degrees of their President's conduct at Paris. Robert Lansing, Wilson's Secretary of State, felt largely neglected in the negotiations and expressed strong objections to his chief's tactics in *The Peace Negotiations* (Cambridge, 1921) and *The Big Four* (Cambridge, 1921). Also critical of Wilson on many points is the account by the head of the American delegation's staff of experts, James T. Shotwell, *At the Paris Peace Conference* (New York, 1937). A more favorable impression of Wilson's role emerges from the papers of the only Republican Peace Commissioner in Allan Nevins's biography, *Henry White* (New York, 1930).

How Wilson appeared to the leaders of other nations at the Conference has been recounted for the French by Georges Clemenceau, *Grandeur and Misery of Victory* (New York, 1930), and André Tardieu, *The Truth About the Treaty* (Indianapolis, 1921); for British views (which differ strongly from those of Keynes and Nicolson) see David Lloyd George, *The Truth About the Peace Treaties* (London, 1938) and Winston Churchill, *The Aftermath, 1918–1928* (New York, 1929).

German charges against the Treaty are set forth (in far less emotional tones than those of *Mein Kampf*) by Karl F. Nowak, *Versailles* (London, 1928). A cogent, brief reply to these charges appears in T. E. Jessop, *The Treaty of Versailles, Was It Just?* (New York, 1942), and a more extended reply is James T. Shotwell's *What Germany Forgot* (New York, 1940).

The adequacy of Wilson's Fourteen Points as a basis for reconstructing a world order is most directly examined in those writings which assess the Treaty of Versailles against a broad historical perspective. E. H. Carr makes severe and far-reaching criticisms of the "reactionary" character of the Versailles settlement in two books, *Conditions of Peace* (New York, 1942) and *The Twenty Years Crisis* (London, 1949). A very recent book by L. C. B. Seaman, *From Vienna to Versailles* (New York, 1956), looks at the failings of the 1919 peace from the standpoint of the balance of power. René Albrecht-Carrié reaches more favorable conclusions about the treaty in "Versailles Twenty Years After," *Political Science Quarterly*, 55 (March, 1940), 1–24.

Two articles provide a valuable review

of historical writing on the Peace Conference: R. C. Binkley, "Ten Years of Peace Conference History," *Journal of Modern History*, 1 (Dec., 1929), 607–629; and Paul Birdsall, "The Second Decade of Peace Conference History," *Journal of Modern History*, 11 (Sept., 1939), 362–378.

A good, brief biography of Wilson is H. C. F. Bell's *Woodrow Wilson and the People* (Garden City, 1945). Solely concerned with Wilson's approach to foreign policy, though restricted mostly to the years before 1919, are Harley Notter, *The Origins of the Foreign Policy of Woodrow Wilson* (Baltimore, 1937) and E. H. Buehrig, *Woodrow Wilson and the Balance of Power* (Bloomington, 1955).

Current writings on the principles and requirements of foreign policy have proliferated to an extent unprecedented in American experience. The debate over "realism" versus "idealism" can be followed in a series of three articles: Hans J. Morgenthau, "The Mainsprings of American Foreign Policy: The National Interest vs. Moral Abstractions," *American Political Science Review*, 44 (Dec., 1950), 833–854; the rejoinder by Frank Tannenbaum which is largely reprinted in this volume; and a reply by Morgenthau, "Another Great Debate: The National Interest of the United States," *American Political Science Review*, 46 (Dec., 1952), 961–988. Tannenbaum's "idealist" view is expanded in *The American Tradition in Foreign Policy* (Norman, Okla., 1955) while Morgenthau both expands his "realist" analysis and applies it to contemporary problems in his *In Defense of the National Interest* (New York, 1952). The most extensive effort to trace and to assess "idealist" and "realist" strains in American conceptions of foreign policy is Robert F. Osgood, *Ideals and Self-interest in America's Foreign Relations* (Chicago, 1953). A roundup of views on many of the issues involved in this debate appears in a symposium, "National Interest and Moral Principles in Foreign Policy," *American Scholar*, 18 (Spring, 1949).

Both George F. Kennan and Charles B. Marshall have published series of lectures which draw upon their years of diplomatic experience for provocative critiques of American attitudes toward foreign affairs. See: Kennan, *American Diplomacy*, 1900–1950 (New York, 1950) and *Realities of American Foreign Policy* (Princeton, 1954); Marshall, *The Limits of Foreign Policy* (New York, 1954). For the efforts of two political scientists to make a systematic study of the essential elements in sound foreign policy see E. S. Furniss, Jr., and R. C. Snyder, *An Introduction to American Foreign Policy* (New York, 1955).